What Others Are S̶̶ ... Getting Over St...

"*Getting Over Stage Fright* is a great sequel to Janet's first book, *In The Spotlight*. It deepens and expands upon her earlier work to guide the reader on a journey of personal growth and development. Janet provides a holistic model to help anyone suffering from speaking or performance fear learn some fundamental principles and practices to reduce anxiety as well as become a stronger and more evolved person. This book will surely help anyone who suffers from the fear of public speaking and performing, as well as many others who struggle with any kind of fear and anxiety."

— EDMUND J. BOURNE, PH.D.,
Author of *The Anxiety & Phobia Workbook*

"Janet Esposito's knowledge of the treatment of performance and social anxiety are exceptional. She is clearly an expert in this field. Her newest book, *Getting Over Stage Fright*, really delivers on what the title promises. This book offers readers a fresh, new perspective on how to overcome stage fright and use fear as a catalyst to personal growth and transformation. I recommend this book wholeheartedly not only to those who want to discover a new approach to their fear of speaking or performing but as an excellent resource to healthcare professionals as well."

— MARY GUARDINO,

Founder/Executive Director, Freedom From Fear

"*Getting Over Stage Fright* is a brilliant book that shows Janet Esposito's depth of experience and expertise in the area of public speaking and performing fear. Janet takes a fresh new approach to the problem of performance anxiety. She skillfully helps the reader to work through their fear and to gain a level of mastery and personal growth that goes well beyond what traditional approaches have offered. This book has done more to make me a confident and effective speaker than the hundreds of communication programs I've attended."

— MOE ABDOU,
Founder, Learn from My Life

"My colleague Janet Esposito has written an extraordinary book at a time when we need it most. If you have an idea, a solution, a process that helps others, a business that needs clients or a career that needs a boost and you are not speaking or presenting due to stage fright, listen to me-buy this book, now. The world needs to hear you and *Getting Over Stage Fright* will show you how easy it can be."

— DIANNE LEGRO,
International speaker, author, top speaking coach
Founder, Speaking Success Today

"Fear can be a powerful catalyst for personal growth and transformation or a crippling agent, preventing you from achieving what's most important. In her latest book, Janet Esposito shows you how to use your mind, body, and spirit to work with, rather than against, your fear of public speaking. This holistic guide will serve as your ally and coach, helping you transform into a speaker who thrives in the spotlight."

— LARINA KASE,
Author of *The Confident Leader: How the Most Successful People Go from Effective to Exceptional*, and the *New York Times* bestseller *The Confident Speaker*

"If you are serious about not letting stage fright keep you from your dreams, this is the book to read. Janet Esposito has a unique talent for blending some of the most practical advice I have ever heard with what I can only describe as genuine wisdom. She is a teacher of the highest caliber."

— THOM RUTLEDGE,
Author of *Embracing Fear: How to Turn What Scares Us Into Our Greatest Gift*

"As someone who has been a professional public speaker for over 15 years I know how essential public speaking skills are to one's success. Unfortunately, many people have such a fear of speaking they limit their opportunities both personally and professionally.

A great solution for anyone who has even the slightest fear of public speaking is Janet Esposito's book *Getting Over Stage Fright*. A great compliment to her first book, *In the Spotlight*, Janet goes deeper into the process of what it takes to deliver a stellar presentation. *Getting Over Stage Fright* is perfect for anyone who wants to overcome their fear once and for all and be one who is known to Thrive in the Spotlight. I highly recommend this book."

— KATHLEEN GAGE,
The Street Smarts Marketer™, Internet marketing advisor

"Perhaps you think you need a book sub-titled, "The 10 Best Tips for Better Performance." Think again. If we can shift our stance about our place in the world, if we can accept all parts of ourselves into one whole and integrated person, there is no stopping our human spirit, innovation and drive. The changes that will last a lifetime are simple, but they aren't about making eye contact with your audience. All this you will discover in *Getting Over Stage Fright*. Get ready to be surprised and relieved at where these pages will carry you."

— REID WILSON, PH.D.,
Author of *Don't Panic: Taking Control of Anxiety Attacks*

GETTING OVER STAGE FRIGHT

A *new* approach to resolving your fear of public speaking and performing

JANET ESPOSITO, MSW

Love Your Life

LOVE YOUR LIFE PUBLISHING, INC • St. Louis, MO

Copyright © 2009 Janet Esposito.

Published by Love Your Life Publishing, Inc
7127 Mexico Road, Suite 121
Saint Peters, MO 63376
1-800-930-3713

ISBN: 978-1-934509-27-2
Library of Congress Control Number: 2009933059

Printed in the United States of America
First Printing August 2009

Author Photo by Wendy Carlson, www.wendycarlson.com
Cover and design by Sarah Van Male, www.cyanotype.ca

GETTING OVER STAGE FRIGHT

A *new* approach to resolving your fear
of public speaking and performing

*To my husband, Rich, and our beautiful golden retriever, April,
who gave me the time and space to write*

To my family, who provided the foundation for my love of learning

*To the many authors and teachers I have learned from, for their
guidance and support along the way*

*To my clients and students, who allowed me to share what
I have learned on my journey*

CONTENTS

ACKNOWLEDGEMENTS

I DEEPLY APPRECIATE THE MANY PEOPLE WHO HAVE SUPPORTED, encouraged, and inspired me to write this book. I would first like to thank my workshop and coaching clients, as the value they report receiving from my work inspired me to share the information I have to offer on a broader scale in the form of a second book. I extend a special heartfelt thanks to the nine people who shared their challenges and successes to help inspire others by generously contributing to the Pure Inspiration section.

I was also strongly encouraged by the many positive reviews of my first book and reports of the value that book has had in many people's lives. I thank all those who took time to submit reviews, making *In The SpotLight* an Amazon bestseller in the category of public speaking for many years now. Knowing that my work was well received and valued by many people has provided the extra impetus I needed to devote time and energy to writing another book.

I am deeply grateful to Emma Swaisland and Jenny Ng of Capstone Publishing, of John Wiley & Sons, Ltd. in the United Kingdom, who recognized the value of my book for an international audience. They initiated the process that led to *In The SpotLight* being published in the United Kingdom and marketed throughout Europe and other parts of the world. I am also deeply grateful to Barbara Kujawska and Dominika Kobiela-Lesniewska of Helion SA Publishing Group in Poland for moving forward on the translation of *In The SpotLight* into Polish. I appreciate their seeing the potential of my work to help the Polish people, which has been particularly meaningful, given that this happens to be my family's cultural background. All of this has further validated the value of my work and inspired me to want to offer more.

I extend my deepest thanks to my colleagues who generously agreed to endorse my book. I know how precious time is and I greatly appreciate their taking their time to support and affirm my work. I want to express special thanks to Kathleen Gage for enthusiastically supporting and promoting my book and Moe Abdou for being an especially strong advocate of my work.

I also thank my dear friends who expressed much interest and enthusiasm on hearing I was writing this book, as well as those who read and offered comments on the first draft, including Rosemary Flannery, Sharon McQuaide, Diane Wirz, Ginger Blume, Sue Casale, Cathy Lipper, and Karen Judd. I also deeply appreciate the assistance of Randy Lee, Tammy Hardisty, Janice Creighton, and Mary Monagan, who have all supported me in countless ways, making it possible for me to find the time and energy for writing.

I would like to express my deepest thanks to Lynne Klippel of Love Your Life Publishing for her incredible kindness, support, and enthusiasm in capably moving my book through the many steps of the publishing process. I also want to extend my appreciation to her partner, Christine Kloser, for her behind the scenes support of this project. I extend a warm thanks to Carolyn Bond for contributing her special talent with editing, as well as her supportive and affirming style, to allow this book to be at its very best. And my deepest appreciation goes to Sarah Van Male for using her amazing talent to create a cover and interior design that houses my book beautifully.

I thank all of the authors and teachers I have had the opportunity to learn from over the years, who have generously shared their knowledge and experience for the benefit of others. I give special thanks to my yoga teachers, Glenn Tucker and Natasha Raymond, who have offered such tremendous wisdom and skill and who I have learned a great deal from.

Finally, I express my deepest appreciation to my Aunt Pat, who has been a consistent positive presence in my life and very much of a parent figure, guiding and supporting me in countless ways.

ABOUT THE AUTHOR

JANET ESPOSITO, MSW, IS A LICENSED CLINICAL SOCIAL WORKER and has been in practice for over twenty-four years as a psychotherapist. In 1998 Janet began to specialize in helping people overcome their fear of public speaking and performing. She started her No More Stage Fright workshops, which drew people from all parts of the country and abroad to the safe and supportive group environment Janet provides to help people who share this challenge.

Janet's first book, *In The SpotLight: Overcome Your Fear of Public Speaking and Performing*, was published in 2000 and has been an Amazon bestseller for over six years. John Wiley & Sons, Ltd, published a U.K. edition in 2008 and has been marketing the book in Europe and other parts of the world. A Polish translation is in process and a Portuguese translation will soon be underway.

Janet co-created a CD, *In The SpotLight: Guided Exercises to Create a Calm and Confident State of Mind, Body, & Spirit While Speaking or Performing*, which has helped many people to apply the principles and practices she teaches. Janet also does individual phone coaching with people throughout the United States and abroad on both an as-needed and a regular basis, and enjoys guiding and supporting people as they face challenges with speaking or performing, as well as helping them apply the principles she teaches in other areas of their lives.

To reach Janet to set up a consultation or to give her feedback after reading this book, email her at **jesposito@performanceanxiety.com** or call her at 860–210–1499. Visit Janet's web site at **www.performanceanxiety.com** to receive a special bonus of tips to help you create comfort, calm, and confidence before, during, and after speaking or performing events.

PREFACE

SEVEN YEARS AFTER MY FIRST BOOK CAME OUT ON THE SUBJECT of fear of public speaking and performing I woke up with my intuition telling me that it was time to start writing again. While I felt excitement about this idea, it also took me by surprise, as I had no clear intention to write another book. Once some of the excitement wore off, I started to feel stress and pressure about starting a big project like this. In recent years I had been making attempts to simplify my life and to be more aware of my tendency to overextend myself. I was finally beginning to lighten the load, and I didn't particularly want to take on another project that required a great deal of time and effort.

The readiness to move forward with another book and the simultaneous reluctance to do so finally reconciled within me, and I started writing again. I acknowledged my strong desire to share what I had learned in recent years with others who have faced similar challenges with fear of public speaking and performing. I also acknowledged that I could give myself permission to be less driven to complete the task within a certain time frame and, instead, let the creative journey unfold in its own time and way, even if this book took a couple years to complete (which it did, I might add).

This book offers a holistic approach to managing, and ultimately transforming, feelings of fear and anxiety by offering a broad range of ideas and practices at the levels of body, mind, and spirit. Though I have divided the book into these three sections, with relevant chapters in each section, there is overlap between the sections and many of the chapters, and ultimately all of the material taken together forms a unified whole. Some ideas and practices will appeal to you more than others, and what most draws your interest and attention may change over time. There is no need to believe in or apply everything I have included. What is most important is that you listen to and trust your inner guidance as to what you most need at any given moment.

I have arranged the body, mind, and spirit sections in a way that allows you to focus on a particular section, or specific chapters within a section, that are most helpful to you. While you can choose a particular section or select chapters without having to read through the book from start to finish, I encourage you to take the time to read through the whole book first, and then go back and select the chapters that are most helpful to you for ongoing reinforcement of the principles and methods.

Each chapter includes a guiding intention to support and encourage a more positive outlook and vision of what is possible and also a suggested affirmation to help focus your mind on the positive message within that chapter. Please feel free to change the language or content of these intentions and affirmations so they resonate better with you, or not use them at all if they don't work for you. Thinking about positive intentions and affirmative thoughts from time to time throughout the day—and creating positive emotions as you visualize manifesting these intentions and affirmations—is a powerful way to focus your mind and connect to a deeper creative source within you. This activity is like planting seeds in the fertile soil of the subconscious mind—it paves the way for a good harvest as you take positive actions to bring about what you most desire.

At the end of each chapter I suggest a practice session to support an active approach to creating positive change. As we all know, insight and understanding alone rarely create change that is deep and lasting. Change happens by consciously applying our new understanding with patience and persistence as we begin to challenge our habitual, conditioned patterns of thought, feeling, and behavior. As we dismantle our old patterns, we gradually open up to a new way of relating to ourselves and to our fear and a new way of being out in the world. Practice falls within the realms of Inner Work and Outer Work, where Inner Work encourages the internal process of change and Outer Work allows us to apply those inner changes in real life situations. Inner and Outer Work complement one another and are equally important. Working with both areas creates a powerful synergy to propel the change process forward.

This book presents many ideas for approaching public speaking or performing challenges in a positive and powerful way and for building a stronger inner foundation to face these challenges. I encourage you to pick and choose among them to create your own personal formula of what works best for you. Of course, it is one thing to know what to do and another to apply what you know. I encourage you to consciously focus on applying what you are learning to manage, reduce, and ultimately transform your fear and anxiety. At the same time, I invite you to be accepting and kind toward yourself at times when you fall short of your desired outcome.

Changing ingrained, conditioned patterns of reactions is not so easy and takes much determination. It is often an up-and-down journey—we gradually make forward movement over time, with occasional setbacks along the way. I encourage you to keep a speaking or performing journal to log your experiences before, during, and after any speaking or performing events. This useful tool allows you to track and reflect on how you are doing and learn what is working for you, what is not working for you, and what changes you need to focus on to make further progress. It is most helpful if you do this self-reflection in a supportive and nonjudgmental way.

A checklist of helpful tips to help you reduce and manage fear and build calm and confidence before, during, and after a speaking or performing challenge is available on my web site: **www.performanceanxiety.com**.

The final section of this book is titled "Pure Inspiration" and includes inspirational personal accounts by clients and students of mine who have achieved success by applying what they have learned from my first book and from workshops and coaching sessions. This section was inspired by the "Pure Inspiration" column in my newsletter and my belief that we are encouraged and supported in our own vision of what is possible by hearing the stories of others who have made the changes that we aspire to make in our own lives. I want to share the inspiration that I have felt as I have watched clients and students create positive and empowering experiences with speaking and performing as they apply what they have been learning.

Albert Einstein once said, "Problems cannot be solved at the same level of awareness that created them." In order to get over stage fright and resolve our fear of public speaking and performing we need to adopt a new approach. We need to increasingly move away from our habitual, conditioned, fear-based reactions and make more conscious, self-directed choices in how we think about and respond to the situations that most challenge us. This deeper change process generally happens gradually over time and requires much inner support, patience, and perseverance as we go through the ups and downs of the learning process. Many people want change to be quick and easy and often become frustrated and discouraged when their change process is not progressing according to their hopes and expectations of consistent, steady, fast-moving progress toward their goals.

Reacting with frustration and discouragement only serves to complicate and undermine your attempts at change. Instead, we need to have realistic expectations for change, which means we have to accept the ups and downs as a normal part of the process and support ourselves each step along the way. We need to learn to accept any setbacks as a natural part of the change process and learn what we can from these experiences whenever they happen. This helps us to become more resilient as we keep our focus on moving forward despite any obstacles along our path rather than feel discouraged or defeated. Learning how to be resilient and bounce back quickly is a very important skill to master and we can practice building this skill anytime we have setbacks or when things don't go as we had hoped for.

It is helpful to see each challenge as an opportunity to practice applying the new skills we are learning and not as a test of our success or a race to see how quickly we can get to the finish line. We need to allow the process to unfold in its own time and way as we work on applying our new approach to the best of our ability at any given moment. Each difficult moment along the path can be approached as an invitation to practice gently supporting and encouraging yourself when the going gets rough, rather than turning against yourself in frustration when you feel you are not meeting up to your own expectations of yourself.

People often tell me they wish they could learn to be more comfortable in their own skin in front of groups. The holistic approach presented in this book has the potential to move you in this direction as you apply these skills over time. Some of the richer benefits of working with your fear in a conscious, evolved way are a growing self-awareness and a deeper acceptance and appreciation of yourself. Approaching your fear in this new way allows you to be more comfortable with presenting yourself in an authentic way and less concerned with what others think of you or how they might judge you.

You may have picked up this book solely for the purpose of learning some quick tips for dealing with your fear of public speaking or performing. If that is the case, I am sure you will find many useful ideas that will help you. It is my hope that you will become interested in going even further and embrace some of these ideas as part of a longer-range, deeper, and broader change process leading to greater self-discovery and personal growth. Further, it is my hope that you can use this greater self-understanding and personal development to make conscious choices that help you to grow and evolve your unique potential in this lifetime.

Approaching Fear as an Invitation to Personal Growth

IT SEEMS LIKE QUITE A STRETCH TO THINK THAT OUR FEAR OF public speaking and performing can actually be a blessing in our lives. That sounds like a big dose of positive thinking—an attempt to be the eternal optimist trying to find the silver lining in a difficult and often painful experience of personal suffering. I am the last person to deny how challenging and agonizing this fear can be for those who suffer from it, having been there myself and having heard the stories of hundreds of fellow sufferers over the years.

At the same time, there is a hidden side to this fear, which you can only discover when you stop running from it and finally face the "monster in the closet." I have personally experienced, and have seen with many coaching clients and workshop participants, how approaching this fear in an adaptive way can lead to unexpected and far-reaching gifts. For me and many others, this fear has served as a "wake-up call"—an invitation to pay closer attention and look more deeply at ourselves and our lives and to learn some profound lessons in the process. The way to discover what our fear has to teach us is to stop seeing it as the enemy and instead begin to be curious about what valuable lessons it offers.

It takes quite a shift in perspective not to see this fear, and the associated symptoms that accompany it, as our enemy. We have spent years fighting it, running from it, trying to control it and feeling it has controlled us, and trying to conquer it and feeling it has won out over us. We have seen our fear as the thing that has stood in our way, robbing us of the level of career success, happiness, self-confidence, and peace of mind we so desire and preventing us from reaching our personal potential as a human being. We have cursed our fear for making us feel so weak and helpless, hidden it from others as our shameful secret, and spent many sleepless nights hoping, wishing, and praying it would go away. So how can we possibly see our fear as anything but our enemy?

I have heard it said that the most difficult people and circumstances are our greatest teachers. When life offers us people and circumstances that are easy and pleasant, we certainly relish them and wish life could always be this way. We come to expect that life should always run smoothly and be the way we want it to be, and we may get quite disgruntled when life presents us with frustrations and obstacles instead. Many of us who suffer from this fear have been high achievers, able to move past most obstacles in our path through a combination of determination and hard work. In fact, as we successfully negotiated the personal and professional challenges along the way, our sense of personal power and being in control of ourselves and our lives has been strongly reinforced.

Our experience of the depth and breadth of this fear has challenged how we see ourselves at the very core and has exposed us to a deep vulnerability we are not used to feeling. We have found it hard to accept ourselves as having this level of fear and vulnerability and, perhaps even more difficult to bear, possibly being seen by others as a person who feels so vulnerable and afraid. We have come to see our fear as a personal weakness and believe we will be judged by others as weak and lacking if our fear and vulnerability become exposed.

Yet our fear has also forced us to pay attention to our inner life in a way that other things have not. When our lives are working smoothly and predictably, it is easy to sail along and not question anything. This fear has stopped us in our tracks and, in doing so, has given us the opportunity to pause and take stock of ourselves and our lives. It is an invitation to become more conscious of patterns in our personality and approach to life that might not be serving us well. It is an opportunity to create a deeper understanding of ourselves, others, and our worldview. It is up to us how far we take this self-discovery, but however far that is, it is always an invitation to grow and evolve as a human being.

In order to learn the lessons that this fear has to teach us we have to change the way we approach it. Rather than try to control and conquer it, we have to learn to accept our fear—even befriend it, be curious about it, and listen for the lessons it offers. Paradoxically, the more we let go of our need to conquer our fear, and instead make peace with this vulnerable part of ourselves, the more the fear eases naturally on its own. We learn how to not be afraid of the fear and how to feel safe and grounded in the midst of feeling fearful. Instead of further fueling the fear with our distressed and anxious reactions when it arises, we learn to relax, accept what is happening, and "ride the wave," all of which begins to shift and transform the energy of fear.

It is important to recognize fear as a natural part of the human condition and not view it as a personal weakness or failing. We need to learn to let go of our strivings toward perfection and accept ourselves as less-than-perfect human beings, realizing we are no better and no worse than others. Many of us are not used to feeling humbled in this way, as we are accustomed to taking pride in the many achievements and successes we have experienced in our lives. It takes humility to accept our imperfections and not feel embarrassed by them. It seems that many of our greatest leaders have been among the most humble people, who accept and appreciate their basic humanness even when others hold them in such high esteem and expect great things of them.

We often have the illusion that others "have it all together" when they appear to be confident and self-assured in their personal style. We may especially envy those who appear that way when speaking or performing, desperately wishing we could be that way. The truth is, we really have no idea how someone is feeling deep within themselves or what their life is really like, based on how they present themselves in public. Most people keep their personal problems and challenges hidden from view, other than perhaps from their closest confidants. Even if someone appears calm, confident, and self-assured as a speaker or performer, the person's public image may or may not accurately reflect his or her inner world and life experience.

Rather than make assumptions about people based on surface impressions, it is more useful to acknowledge the truth that you have no idea what their lives are like below the surface and behind the scenes. Rest assured that everyone has their fair share of imperfections, feelings of vulnerability, and challenges in response to some aspect of life, whether it is apparent or not. One surprising, and reassuring, revelation that has occurred over and over again in my workshops over the years is the discovery that others cannot detect our fear and vulnerability as much as we may think (and often not at all). People are amazed by this, given how strong the feelings can be and how intense the experience is for the person going through such inner turmoil.

Whatever your own inner struggle is, and however it came to be, the point is that you are not transparent and neither is anyone else. Even if someone detects something in you, they have no way of knowing what exactly is going on or the depth and breadth of the fear and vulnerability you might be experiencing. The other important point to recognize is that there is nothing wrong with you for having these feelings, as no one is immune to feeling fear and vulnerability as they deal with especially challenging life issues and problems. Rather than fighting against or running away from these feelings, and judging ourselves for having them, it is much wiser to allow and accept them as part of our human experience.

Some people have spoken of "the imposter syndrome," feeling they are presenting themselves as a fraud if others perceive them to be confident and self-assured when they are actually experiencing such intense fear and anxiety. This can be said of just about everyone, as most people keep their deepest vulnerabilities private, sharing these only with those closest to them or perhaps with no one at all. The idea of being an "imposter" or "fraud" suggests a deliberate attempt to deceive others for your own gain, and this is just not the case with those who are trying to cope with a speaking or performing fear and doing the best they can under difficult circumstances.

Our cultural conditioning encourages us to assume and expect things of each other based on superficial impressions. If people assume and expect things of you based on how you appear on the surface, know that you are not being an imposter if the deeper truth is different. Likewise, others are not being imposters if they keep a part of their lives hidden from public view. We are all trying to cope with our life challenges in a culture that doesn't encourage that depth of honesty and disclosure, and it is not a personal statement about you if your outer presentation differs from your inner experience.

When we are feeling so vulnerable, and in a state of heightened fear and anxiety, it is as though we are in a trance and we can easily distort our perceptions of ourselves and others. We often regress into feeling like a small, frightened child and disconnect from our usual adult functioning. We may feel different, separate, lost, and alone. Our self-preoccupation and narrow view further fuel feelings of isolation and alienation, which feed the cycle of fear and self-doubt.

When we are able to step back and challenge our belief in these fear-based distortions, we are able to see more of the truth about ourselves and others. As we look more deeply at what is true, we are able to see and feel the humanity in the room and to realize we are all on this journey together. It helps us realize that people are much more alike than different in the challenges we face as human beings. It allows us to not get intimidated by those who hold positions of power or prestige, or to think lesser of those who don't hold positions of status. And it invites us to open up at a heart level and feel our connection to others rather than experience ourselves as different, separate, and alone.

To heal the roots of our speaking or performing fear requires a paradigm shift—a radically different approach. It is best to work on all three levels of body, mind, and spirit as we create a new way to manage and transform our fear. We can ground ourselves in our bodies and thereby create a strong and stable foundation within ourselves to turn to in moments of fear. We can work with our mind so it comes to serve us better as an ally rather than work against us, as is so often the case. And, to complete the spectrum of potential healing and transformation from this fear, we can tap into the wisdom, truth, and heightened awareness of our spiritual nature. It is by tapping into this realm that we can cultivate our deepest growth and highest potential as we learn to move away from our individual, self-focused ego concerns and bring down the barrier between ourselves and others that keep us trapped in fear.

In healing and transforming our feelings of fear and vulnerability, we are also creating the potential to deepen and expand our conscious awareness of ourselves, others, and the world around us. The fear is an invitation to pay attention to the unconscious, conditioned ways in which many of us are living and discover how to live a more conscious life. In gaining wisdom and skill in how we approach our fear, we can also become more wise and skillful in how we approach life itself.

SECTION ONE

BODY

CHAPTER ONE

Inhabiting
Your Body

MANY OF US LIVE IN OUR MINDS A GOOD DEAL OF THE TIME. We barely notice our bodies unless they are calling our attention through aches and pains, fatigue, or other symptoms of physical discomfort or distress. At those times we may become frustrated, concerned, anxious, or annoyed with our bodies for showing signs that something is not right with us, and we quickly try to remedy the discomfort or distress so we can get on with the business of our lives without this interference. This is especially the case when our bodies express symptoms of heightened anxiety and fear, as our discomfort can become very intense and frightening when we feel a loss of control inside of ourselves. Our intense physical symptoms often lead us to feel betrayed by our bodies and fearful of the power our bodies have to instantaneously seize control and render us feeling powerless over the forces within us.

At other times we may be more aware and tuned in to our bodies, such as when we are experiencing pleasure in the body. In between the experiences of painful and pleasurable physical sensations, which draw our awareness and attention to the body, there are often long gaps when we feel disconnected from our physical bodies. The world that we inhabit much of the time is the world of the mind—the world of concepts and ideas, information and knowledge, thoughts and beliefs. It is quite easy to get lost in thought, and lost in information overload, almost forgetting that we are connected to our bodies unless they call out for our attention.

It is especially easy to become disconnected from our bodies when we are living in a fast-paced, rushed, and driven way. Our bodies tend to almost disappear from our awareness when we are striving to keep up with ongoing demands and pressures in our lives. When we get caught up in our busy minds and the hurried pace of living, we can easily lose touch with the vital life force within our bodies. We can also lose our sense of grounding in the world, particularly when we are in stressful and difficult circumstances or situations we perceive as threatening. It is very important, then, that we create a close and supportive relationship with the body and discover how it can provide a steady anchor for us to weather the stormy times in life, as well as a vehicle to feel more grounded and stable in responding to day-to-day stresses.

Most of us are not aware of the ongoing disconnect between our minds and bodies unless it is made obvious by an "out of body" experience, the kind that can occur when we are feeling very threatened in a situation of speaking or performing. Many people have commented on this experience, which feels like we have left our bodies and are going through the motions of speaking or performing but are not really "there." This is a more extreme version of the subtle disconnect between body and mind that we often operate with as we navigate the normal stresses and pressures of our daily lives.

Living much of our time in our minds without feeling grounded and con-nected in our bodies creates cumulative levels of tension, stress, anxiety, and alienation from ourselves. It also does not allow us to experience the full depth and breadth of our own aliveness and the aliveness in the world around us.

In order to create a place of safety and refuge within our bodies, we need to develop a close and trusting relationship with our bodies and learn to inhabit them more fully on a daily basis. We can learn to "come home" to the body as a place of protection and support at times when we are feeling overwhelmed and afraid. We can learn to trust that our bodies can provide a safe haven in times of stress and turbulence. And we can discover how to stay connected to our bodies to be more anchored in the present moment rather than living in the often scary projections and distortions of the mind based in the past and the future.

Eckhart Tolle, in *A New Earth*, states that one way to inhabit your body is to create more awareness and connection with what he calls your "inner body" and the amazing aliveness that is going on inside of you at every moment. He suggests you first pay attention to your hands and, then, with eyes open or closed, begin to feel the life energy that exists within your hands. Extend this practice to other parts of your body, and then to your body as a whole, which will help you to connect more with the aliveness going on deep within you. As you become more conscious of this inner aliveness, you can begin to place a part of your attention on your inner body experience while you are also involved in daily activities. He states, "Whenever you 'inhabit' your body in this way, it serves as an anchor for staying present in the Now. It prevents you from losing yourself in thinking, in emotions, or in external situations."

There are many other ways to create a deeper connection with your body and to feel grounded and supported by it. I will be reviewing some of them in the following pages. There is no one right or perfect way to do this. I will share with you some of the practices that have worked well for me, and for my clients, though there are many other useful methods to create this grounded and supported feeling. I invite you to stay open to discovering the ways that work best for you to deepen your awareness of, connection with, and trust in your own body.

Guiding Intention: I connect with awareness of my body each day and discover ways my body can provide me with stability and support.

Affirmative Thought: I "come home" to my body and find a place of safety, support, and refuge.

Practice: Sit or lie down in a quiet, comfortable space without distractions. Take a few deep, relaxing breaths and allow your mind to settle. Imagine the feeling of "coming back home" to your body, and experience a place of safety and support deep within your body, where you are protected from the stresses and pressures of the outside world. Feel this place in your body as your own safe haven that is always there waiting for you to come home to whenever you need to feel safe and protected. You may want to quietly say the words *come back home* as you connect to this place deep within you. See if you can stay connected to this place within you for a few moments and revisit it each day as a way of developing a supportive and trusting relationship with your body. When you make this a daily practice, it is easier to remember to come back home to your safe haven in times of heightened pressure and stress in your life.

Now, close your eyes and imagine coming back home to this safe haven when you are waiting for a speaking or performing event to begin, or in the midst of this challenge, and feeling very anxious and afraid. Feel the safety and protection as you connect to this place of refuge within you. Continue to practice coming back home to this safe haven whenever you are feeling fear and anxiety and experience the calming effects of connecting with this protected place within you.

CHAPTER TWO

Learning How to
Ground Yourself

DISCOVERING HOW TO GROUND OURSELVES BEGINS WITH MOVING our attention and energy down from our busy minds into our bodies. We feel more grounded when we experience the stability and strength of our physical bodies and the sensation of our feet planted firmly on the earth. We feel more grounded when we focus on our breath—allowing slow, full inhalations and exhalations as we gently guide the breath as it moves through our bodies—and when we bring our attention to the different parts of our bodies and feel the sensations and aliveness within us.

By contrast, there are many things that can lead to the experience of not feeling grounded, a feeling many of us know all too well. It is easy to lose our equilibrium as we face the pressures and demands of our lives, and we are especially vulnerable to losing a steady, grounded feeling when we are confronted with particularly stressful life events, such as when we are facing speaking or performing challenges.

At these stressful times, our energy and attention are highly charged in our busy minds, which are projecting worry and concern about our ability to manage the challenges we face. Our minds tend to speed up and race with thoughts that further fuel a feeling of threat and alarm. This process activates the fight or flight reaction in our bodies, and we begin to physically experience that familiar agitated feeling as our nervous systems prepare for a perceived emergency. As we lose touch with that grounded, safe place in our bodies, our minds get more alarmed and the stress response activates even further. We are caught in a highly charged feedback loop between mind and body, and we feel ourselves very quickly spiraling downward as we experience a profound loss of control.

One thing that brings us back to feeling grounded is to slow all systems down. True danger and emergency dictate the need for fast, immediate reactions to keep us safe. When we consciously and deliberately slow down our bodies and minds, we are giving our nervous systems the message that no true emergency is going on. Our nervous systems respond by calming down the fight or flight reaction. Once we slow things down, the body relaxes and calms itself more naturally and easily, which has a direct effect on quieting and settling the mind as well.

It is helpful to become aware of the hurried pace at which many of us move in day-to-day life and to start there to slow things down a bit by creating moments of pause and relaxation. Some have called our pace of living "hurry sickness," as we rush through life trying to fit everything in—multitasking, checking things off our "to do" lists, and impatiently making our way from one thing to the next. This fast pace of life, and the feeling of always having more to do than time allows for, creates an ongoing source of stress and tension that builds over time, often without our being aware of the toll it is taking. We lose our sense of life balance and deplete our emotional reserves, making it even more difficult to feel grounded when higher level challenges come our way.

Whenever our minds and bodies begin to race and we lose the feeling of being grounded, one of the best things we can do is to pause for a moment and breathe slowly, deeply, and fully. This simple action allows us to take a step back from whatever is going on, slow everything down, and regroup. Taking a pause interrupts the pattern of emotional reactivity and helps us to regain our equilibrium. It gives us an opportunity to make a conscious choice to step back from whatever negative cycle is beginning. Pausing and taking a few slow, deep, full breaths is a powerful way to immediately ground and steady ourselves in the moment by connecting with our body in a calming and supportive way.

We are all familiar with that racing, rushed feeling that surges within us when we are facing a speaking or performing challenge, leaving us feeling ungrounded and unsteady in our bodies and minds. When we are in the midst of this fight or flight reaction, our automatic reaction is to speed up even more—to move more quickly, talk more quickly, and react more quickly so we can move through and away from the perceived danger as fast as possible. All of this hurried movement in the body and mind serves to further unsteady us and supports the belief that we are facing an immediate and urgent threat.

To feel more safe and grounded in our bodies, and in our minds, we must slow the body down at the very moment the automatic fight or flight reaction wants to speed us up. This means we need to consciously and deliberately move more slowly, speak more slowly, and respond more slowly. As soon as we begin to slow things down, we begin to feel more safe and grounded. Our bodies and minds begin to relax a bit, and this further supports a feeling of safety, which allows us to start to let down our guard. Consciously pausing and slowing things down—whether we are anticipating a speaking or performing event or are in the midst of such a challenge—helps us to feel safer, calmer, and more grounded. It is a simple yet powerful and immediate way to regain feelings of stability and steadiness when we are feeling highly anxious and afraid.

Guiding Intention: I consciously and deliberately pause and slow things down whenever I feel stress and pressure building inside of me.

Affirmative Thought: I pause and breathe slowly, deeply, and fully whenever I face a speaking (or performing) challenge.

Practice: Take an honest look at your lifestyle and become aware of the patterns of stress and pressure in your life. Consider ways that you may be able to slow down the pace or give yourself moments of respite. Consider how you can build relaxation into your daily life rather than wait for weekend down time or yearly vacations to alleviate any building tension. Also consider creating moments of pause throughout your day, allowing you to step back from the momentum of your activities to breathe, relax, and ground yourself in the present moment.

Increase your awareness of tendencies for your body to speed up and your mind to race when facing speaking or performing challenges. Consciously and deliberately pause and shift your attention to taking full, deep breaths and slowing down your rate of speaking, moving, and responding to whatever is happening within you and around you. Feel the sensation in your feet, anchored firmly on the floor, and the support of the earth below you. Allow your body to relax as you create a foundation of safety and stability within you, and allow your mind to naturally settle as it perceives there is no immediate threat or danger.

CHAPTER THREE

Allowing Your Breath to Calm and Center You

MOST OF US DON'T PAY MUCH ATTENTION TO OUR BREATH. We take it for granted. Yet it is the very thing that keeps us alive moment to moment and supports our physical and emotional equilibrium. The breath is indeed a very powerful force and something we want to consciously work with to help support us when we are anxious or in need of grounding. It provides us with an immediate and readily accessible way to support a foundation of inner calm and balance as we deal with the pressures and demands of our daily lives, as well as when we face the bigger challenges of life.

Relaxation, meditation, and yoga practices—and other methods focused on creating calm and stability—generally use the breath as a focal point for centering, grounding, and stabilizing body and mind. In the practice of meditation, the breath is often used as an anchor, helping to steady, focus, and settle our minds as our thoughts start to pull us in many different directions. The breath becomes a reliable focal point to return to when our minds feel unsettled and get tangled up in a stream of thoughts that pull us toward preoccupation with the past or projections into the future. When we come back to the breath, we come back to the present moment and our minds naturally begin to settle.

In yoga, the breath is considered an integral part of the practice. Breath work supports the release of stored up tensions and areas of constriction in the body and mind. It has been said that when we control the breath, we control the mind. As we deepen and expand our breath, we invite relaxation into the body, and the mind naturally begins to slow down and calm itself. The breath work helps with physical and emotional balance and also invites a deeper connection and unity among body, mind, and spirit. Other forms of breath practice energize and inspire higher levels of awareness and vitality in body, mind, and spirit.

In relaxation and stress management practices, deep breathing is also a central method used to help release stored up tensions and begin to relax the body and mind. Breathing more fully and deeply is an immediate message to the nervous system that it is safe to let down our guard. We begin to soften the constrictions in our bodies and minds, which invites a natural process of relaxation to unfold. The practice of deep breathing also oxygenates our systems and physiologically supports feelings of calm and well-being.

When we are not conscious of our breath and are reacting to situations of stress or perceived threat, our breath constricts and becomes shallow and rapid. Sometimes, when we are especially overwhelmed, we may find ourselves holding our breath as though we are waiting until it is safe to exhale. Such disturbances in our breathing throw our nervous system into high alert and disrupt our physical and emotional equilibrium. It is essential that we consciously guide our breath to help create feelings of inner safety and balance so we are not pulled into an instinctual fight or flight response when there is no real danger or threat in our path.

There are many different ways to work with the breath and many books on the subject. While you may want to learn more about the range of breath practices available, you can also keep it very simple and straightforward. The first thing to do, especially in times of stress, tension, or challenge, is to simply pay attention to your breath. Notice that your breath may start to constrict, become shallow and rapid, or hold onto inhalations without exhaling normally and fully during those times.

If you notice your breath showing signs of distress, begin to gently deepen and expand your breath, being sure each full and complete exhalation is followed by a gentle, full, and deep inhalation. Allow the process to be natural and unforced, as trying too hard to breathe fully and deeply will add further stress and tension to your nervous system.

It is helpful to direct the in-breath into the deep core of your body—to that place in your body that allows you to feel the most grounded. As you inhale, let the front, back, and sides of your torso expand. On the out-breath, imagine releasing and letting go of inner tension and stress with a full and complete exhalation. Let your breathing gradually center and calm you.

You may also want to associate the breath work with counting, calming words or phrases, colors, or visual imagery—additional cues that promote relaxation and safety. Some examples of cues to use while breathing might be:

- a slow count of four on the in-breath and four on the out-breath
- words like "relax," "calm," "peaceful" or phrases like "let go," "breathe and relax," "stay in the present moment"
- visualize your favorite color or the color blue (which represents relaxation), yellow (which encourages optimism), or red (which is associated with increased power)
- use visual imagery, such as a wave gently rolling in and out of the ocean, a puffy white cloud passing slowly through a clear blue sky, a solid oak tree with roots going deep into the ground, or a strong, solid mountain with an unshakable foundation

If you choose to use these or other cues with the breath work, be sure to keep it simple. There are no absolutes on doing breath work, and it is important to experiment to discover what works best for you.

Some people have expressed frustration with the process of deep breathing and have said that they don't find it particularly helpful. Others report that they become more uptight and anxious as they try to breathe more deeply and relax. The key is to be patient and not try too hard or try to get it just right. Feelings of impatience and frustration tend to constrict the breath and make it that much harder to relax.

Deep, diaphragmatic breathing is an important ingredient in calming the body and mind when you feel highly stressed and anxious. I encourage you to practice using your breath as a natural and effective way to calm and relax yourself. It helps to cultivate a practice of deep breathing on a daily basis and not try to learn it when you are in the midst of a stressful situation. This practice builds awareness and skill and allows the breath to come more naturally and easily when you face speaking or performing challenges, or other stressful life circumstances.

Guiding Intention: I breathe deeply and allow my breath to be a reliable source of support to ground me in times of stress and challenge.

Affirmative Thought: I remember to breathe fully and deeply whenever I face speaking (or performing) challenges.

Practice: Focus awareness on your breath each day and notice times when your breath is rapid, shallow, held, or otherwise constricted. In a gentle, natural way, allow your attention to guide your body to deepen and expand the range of your breathing. Allow fullness and completeness in your exhalations and inhalations, and allow the expansion to take place in the front, back, and sides of your body. Breathe deeply into your core and allow your breath to connect with the part of your body where you feel the most grounded and supported. Try using relaxing words or other cues if you would like.

You may want to practice breath work as part of the natural flow of your day or devote focused attention to it at specific times of day. Do what you can to make it a regular part of your life so you more easily remember to turn to your breath and deepen and expand it in times of stress. Before and during a speaking or performing event, pay especially close attention to deepening and expanding your breath. Consider writing a reminder note to yourself to *breathe and relax* while you are in the midst of a speaking or performing challenge.

CHAPTER FOUR

Using Your Posture to Strengthen and Support You

LIKE BREATHING, POSTURE OFTEN RECEIVES LITTLE ATTENTION. Many of us have fallen into long-term patterns of poor posture as our bodies react to the ongoing demands and pressures of life. We contract our bodies in response to stress and carry chronic tension in ways that we are often not aware of. Our shoulders may be hunched over, with our neck jutting forward and our back slouching down into the base of the spine. Our chest may be constricted and sunken inward, and our belly may be tense and tight, obstructing the full expansion of our breath. Our legs and feet may be positioned in ways that do not solidly support the body. Our jaw may be tight and clenched, and our face may carry strain and tension in its expression.

Generally, we are not very aware of the patterns of physical expression we carry in our bodies, yet they can have powerful effects on our state of mind. In the practices of yoga and meditation, as well as other practices that are devoted to creating positive states of body and mind, posture is an important factor that is given conscious attention. One's posture is used to train the body to relax and release pent up tension and the mind to be more aware and alert. Paying conscious attention to improving our posture helps us to support our body and increases our awareness of the strong mind-body connection.

The elements of posture and facial expression that support a more positive state of body and mind include having the shoulders gently pulled back and down in a relaxed and open way; the spine firmly and comfortably erect and aligned; the chest open and expansive and the belly comfortably moved in toward the back; the neck well aligned on top of the spine with the crown of the head held high; a loose, relaxed jaw with the mouth slightly opened; a softening around the eyes and a relaxed, slight smile on the face; and the legs and feet positioned to create a solid, steady foundation at the base of the body, with the feet planted firmly on the ground. These can be practiced when sitting or standing, as well as when we are walking and moving about in our day. It is especially helpful to consciously create a relaxed, supportive, and strengthening posture and facial expression at times of challenge and stress, as well as when we are engaged in daily routines that may invite sloppiness in posture or tension in our facial expression.

Take note of the type of body posture and facial expression that take place when you are anxious and uptight as you face a speaking or performing challenge. Notice how your body and mind feel when you are holding a posture and facial expression that do not support you well. Often this type of body posture and expression reinforce feelings of tightness and tension, lack of inner stability, and loss of strength and confidence.

When we consciously and deliberately alter our posture and facial expression to invite a more relaxed, open, expansive, confident, and strengthening feeling in the body, our minds experience a similar open, uplifted, and empowered feeling. Our bodies and minds have a tightly interconnected feedback loop operating between them, and it makes sense to consciously guide the body to support the mind by paying close attention to how we hold and carry our bodies.

Guiding Intention: I consciously guide my posture and facial expression to be open and relaxed, and to support me in feeling strong and confident.

Affirmative Thought: I feel open, relaxed, strong, and confident in my body when I face speaking (or performing) challenges.

Practice: Pay attention to your body posture and facial expression, both in daily routines of life and at times of stress and challenge. Take particular note of any repetitive patterns in your body and expression that lead you to feel tense or constricted, unsteady or unstable, or that reinforce feelings of loss of confidence, personal power, and vitality.

Close your eyes and imagine being in a speaking or performing event. Assume the body posture and facial expression that is typical for you when you are facing this type of challenge and feel highly anxious and stressed. Notice how this posture and expression make you feel and any effects they have on your feelings of confidence and ease.

Now, shake your body a bit and try again. This time, consciously guide your body to create a posture and facial expression that support an open, relaxed, strong, steady, and confident way of being. Note the difference in this body posture and facial expression and how it makes you feel, both in your body and in your mind.

Practice creating a more relaxed and confident body posture and facial expression in day-to-day life, as well as at times of stress, especially when you are facing a speaking or performing challenge.

CHAPTER FIVE

Relaxing
Your Body

IT IS HELPFUL TO SUPPORT OUR BODIES IN RELEASING STORED-UP tension and learning to relax as we often hold much tightness in our bodies without being aware of it. In fact, it is far more effective to focus on creating a state of relaxation than to try to directly eliminate fear and anxiety. An anxious mind cannot easily remain so anxious when the body is in a state of relaxation. When we practice relaxing and letting go of tension in our bodies, we feel an immediate and direct quieting and settling of our worried and anxious minds.

There are many different ways to relax the body. You may want to experiment with various practices to see what works well for you and your body. You may focus on one type of practice or do a diverse set of practices to promote deep relaxation in the body. Whatever you choose, I encourage you to do it on a daily basis if possible, which allows your body to regularly release built-up tension and invites your body to discover a place of deep relaxation. Doing something daily will help train your body in the practice of relaxing more fully and deeply, which will be especially important when times of stress and pressure come your way.

One of the practices that I, as well as some of my clients, have found deeply relaxing to the body and mind is yoga. There are different types of yoga practice, each having its own particular style, as well as varying levels of practice suited to the skill of the practitioner. Whatever style and level you choose, the practice of yoga encourages a deep body awareness and connection to our physical selves. The varied postures and wide range of movement assist the body in releasing tension and tightness and encourage flexibility and openness. The more gentle postures and their meditative focus invite the body to find its way to a deep state of relaxation. If you are new to yoga, you may want to take a beginner's class to see if this practice interests you. You can also find some good yoga DVDs available to support a home practice.

Some people find they are not drawn to yoga but they discover much value in doing a daily series of stretches to release tension and relax different parts of the body. If this is the case for you, you may want to do some of the standard stretches that many people do to loosen up before, and sometimes after, rigorous exercise. If you are not familiar with these stretches, you can learn them from a book, in consultation with a trainer, or from some other qualified source. An alternative is to lie down for ten to fifteen minutes on a mat and stretch in ways that your body seems to be calling for, being sure to listen closely to your body and only stretching in ways that feel good to you.

Another wonderful type of release and relaxation for the body is massage. There are many different types of massage and other forms of bodywork, ranging from the very gentle touch of healing energy work to rigorous deep tissue massage meant to release deeply conditioned patterns of physical and emotional holding in the body. Here too, you may want to explore the range of what is available to see what suits you best. I have found that massage, and other forms of bodywork, have profound effects in helping release accumulated body tension and find a place of deep peace and relaxation.

Yet another useful relaxation exercise is the body scan. In this practice, you lie quietly in comfortable surroundings and begin to focus attention on each part of your body, starting from your feet and slowly moving up to your head. As you come to each area of the body you imagine softening and loosening that part of the body, inviting and allowing it to feel deeply and comfortably relaxed. Some people find it helpful to repeat a phrase that supports the suggestion for relaxation in each part of the body, such as, "My feet are loose, at ease, and deeply relaxed," "My calves are loose, at ease, and deeply relaxed," "My thighs are loose, at ease, and deeply relaxed." You can choose other calming words that resonate better with you, or use no words at all, in which case your attention is fully on the sensation alone. Some people like to do this exercise to calming, soothing music, which can enhance the process of deeply relaxing the body.

Another well-known relaxation exercise involves progressively creating and holding muscle tension, followed by releasing that tension, as you scan your body. Starting with your feet and toes, intentionally create a moderate level of tension and tightness and hold the tension in that area. After feeling the discomfort, cue yourself with a word or phrase to release and fully let go of the tension and deeply relax that part of the body. Continue slowly moving upward through each part of your body until you reach your face and head, repeating each series of tensing, holding, releasing tension, and relaxing. This exercise provides immediate, direct body awareness as it highlights the contrast between holding tension and releasing and relaxing tension.

Many clients tell me they know they should make time for relaxation, but the pressures and demands of life crowd their schedule and lead them to neglect this aspect of self-care. It is important to not make relaxation just another item on your list of "shoulds" that leaves you feeling badly if you are not starting, or sustaining, this effort. Keep in mind the value of setting aside some time for relaxation, and notice the difference between when you devote time and attention to relaxation and when you let it slide. I have found that for many people, even a few minutes of daily focused attention on deeply relaxing the body can have noticeable effects. It seems that the regularity and quality of daily attention to relaxation can be even more important than carving out a large block of time. As always, do the best you can and try not to make finding time to relax an added stress in your life!

Guiding Intention: I am aware of the tightness and tension in my body, and I devote some time and attention each day to deeply relaxing my body.

Affirmative Thought: I practice releasing tension and relaxing my body whenever I face a speaking (or performing) challenge.

Practice: Consider which practices you feel most drawn to that would help you to release body tension and promote relaxation. Reflect on how to make relaxation a priority and how to make time on a regular basis to engage in some form of relaxation practice, even if it is only for brief periods. See if you can also carve out longer spans of time to go deeper in your relaxation practice when possible. Try not to pressure yourself about this or make it another "should" on your list of things to do. Instead, see this time as a sanctuary that buffers you from the demands of your life and provides a time to nurture and support yourself.

Notice the effects on your body and mind when you are engaging in a practice of relaxation compared to times when you neglect this aspect of self-care. Notice how much more easily relaxation of body and mind come when you are planting and watering the seeds of relaxation on a daily basis. Likely, you will see a noticeable difference and feel drawn to sustaining a regular practice of relaxation. Once you have built skill in training yourself to relax, look for opportunities to practice relaxation in moments of stress and pressure.

Now, close your eyes and imagine approaching a speaking or performing event. Notice how your body starts to tense and tighten as you feel anxious about what is up ahead. Become aware of the tightness in your body and consciously release the tension and relax your body. Observe the difference in how it feels to hold tension and release tension. Notice how creating a more relaxed state in your body naturally helps to ease anxiety. Continue to practice conscious relaxation every time you face a speaking or performing challenge.

CHAPTER SIX

Taking Good Care
of Yourself

WHEN WE GET BUSY, AND CAUGHT UP WITH THE DAILY DEMANDS and responsibilities of life, it is easy to neglect taking good care of ourselves and not make it a priority. The signs of not engaging in good self-care can be subtle and easily overlooked, especially when we are not paying close attention to the messages that our bodies are sending us. It is often not until we feel the cumulative effects of stress and fatigue that we begin to appreciate the importance of better self-care.

Care of the body is an important ingredient of effective stress management, and good self-care works best when you are attentive on a proactive, rather than reactive, basis. Again, it comes back to priorities. When time is tight and many things call for your attention, it is easy to put self-care on the back burner and not take action until your body shows obvious signs of wear and tear. It is much wiser to develop positive self-care habits and practice them on a regular basis, as this supports the foundation of your physical and emotional well-being and helps you to be more resilient in times of stress.

There are many ways to practice good self-care. I will note here a few that I believe are especially valuable in promoting feelings of physical and emotional well-being, as well as increasing our capacity to manage stressful times. As most of us well know, a good diet and regular exercise are basic ingredients in supporting a healthy lifestyle and generally improving mood, confidence, and energy. Perhaps you have already incorporated these two important practices into your life and are reaping their rewards. If you are not practicing positive habits of healthy eating and exercise in a regular and sustained way, rather than coming down hard on yourself, take a step back and try to understand what is getting in your way. Then come up with a realistic plan to better support yourself in these key areas of self-care.

Also note any less than healthy—or downright unhealthy—lifestyle habits you may be engaging in. Paying attention to your caffeine and sugar intake is important, as ingesting these things (especially in larger quantities) can throw off your physical and emotional equilibrium. This is also the case with drinking alcohol in excess, using nicotine, or taking in any other form of mind-altering substance. Often, unhealthy lifestyle habits originate as quick and easy ways to soothe and comfort ourselves in the midst of ongoing stress, as well as numbing our tension in times of high anxiety. While engaging in these habits may, in fact, ease feelings of anxiety and distress, they ultimately disempower you and work against creating the healthy body and mind that can provide a foundation for effective stress management.

Regularly getting a good night's sleep is another key element in good self-care. What a good night's sleep exactly means in terms of quantity and quality of sleep may vary from person to person. Take an honest look at your sleep habits and assess how well they are supporting your physical and emotional well-being. If you find you are not making good sleep a priority for your self-care, you may want to consider making a plan to do better in this area, and then notice the difference in how you feel, both physically and emotionally. Being well-rested has a huge impact on the quality of our lives and in how well we manage times of high anxiety and stress. Often, in the busyness of our lives and our need to attend to pressing responsibilities, it is all too easy to make sleep a low priority. Instead, protect and preserve your sleep so you have the inner reserves to support you in better meeting life's demands.

Another aspect of good self-care is simply taking a break from the pressures and demands of life. Making time for recreation, pleasure, laughter, and joy not only rests and relaxes the body and mind; it also promotes a healthy perspective on life. One of the signs of good mental health is the ability to lighten up, to laugh and not take yourself or life too seriously. Many of us have a hard time lightening up, especially when we are under pressure, and our overly serious mindset often leads us to lose perspective and feel weighed down and burdened by the demands in our lives. Identifying what brings you laughter and joy, and engaging in it on a regular basis, is an antidote to an overly serious mind, reminding us of the lighter and more comic side of ourselves and our lives.

However you choose to practice good self-care, it is worth making it a priority so it gets daily time and attention in the midst of the pressing demands of your life. Taking good care of your body calms and strengthens your mind. Feeding your soul with positive, uplifting experiences helps you feel more grounded and alive in your body and connects you to the core of who you really are. When your daily lifestyle nurtures the body, mind, and spirit connection, you are better equipped to handle the everyday stresses as well as the larger challenges that come your way.

While it is ideal to practice good self-care regularly, it is especially important the days before a speaking or performing challenge. Practicing good self-care builds confidence and belief in yourself. It is a profound message of love and kindness, a message that you are worth caring for.

Guiding Intention: I am attentive to doing those things each day that support the health and wellness of my body, mind, and spirit.

Affirmative Thought: I am building a stronger foundation to meet my speaking (or performing) challenges as I devote time and attention each day to practicing good self-care.

Practice: Reflect on your current level of self-care and your self-care history over the course of your adult life. Note the practices that have worked well for you and those you have been able to sustain over time. Note any that worked well in the past and you have not sustained. Reflect on why this may be and, if you feel inclined to pick up any of these practices again, what adjustments you may need to make to maintain them.

Note areas where you are not taking such good care of yourself, and reflect on why this may be and the effects it is having on your body, mind, and spirit. Be kind and forgiving toward yourself on this one, as it is not meant to fuel frustration or upset with yourself.

Finally, after taking an honest look at your lifestyle practices, create a realistic, manageable plan of where to start giving more time and attention in the areas that need them. Rather than trying to change several habits at once, start in an area that feels doable as a first step in this effort. Then build upon this positive momentum over time, creating lifestyle habits that support your well-being and letting go of negative habits that diminish your health and wellness. And be sure to take exceptionally good care of yourself as much as possible in the days before a speaking or performing event.

CHAPTER SEVEN

Accepting Feelings of Fear and Anxiety

WE ALL WANT TO FEEL COMFORTABLE IN OUR OWN SKIN, AND we are often quickly unnerved when highly uncomfortable feelings and sensations arise within our bodies and minds. We tend to have a particularly strong aversion to the feelings and sensations brought on by high levels of fear and anxiety. Our *Oh no, here it comes again* button gets pushed as we feel ourselves rapidly heading toward the slippery slope of experiencing loss of control. We become tense and frightened as we brace ourselves for the often abrupt and rapid decline in our physical and emotional equilibrium.

This reaction is completely understandable, based on our history of experiencing an intense feeling of loss of control in the midst of our fear and anxiety. We became sensitized to these feelings and developed a conditioned response that activates any time we feel at risk of feeling so vulnerable and overwhelmed again, especially in the public eye.

While an episode of intense fear and anxiety is a deeply uncomfortable and unpleasant experience, it is our fearful alarm reactions and avoidant behaviors that create the bigger problem for us. These reactions and behaviors add power, energy, and drama to the fear and anxiety and lead to the vicious cycle of "fearing the fear itself."

It is not easy to calm our fear and anxiety once it has become a strongly conditioned response to something, such as public speaking or performing, that we have come to perceive as highly threatening. We are hard-wired to react quickly, intensely, and instinctively to protect ourselves from anything that might endanger our physical or psychological survival and well-being. While it feels unnatural—and runs contrary to our instinctive impulse to protect ourselves—we must learn to be open and relaxed when these unsettling feelings and body sensations arise. As we learn to soften toward these feelings and sensations—and allow, accept, and ultimately befriend our fear and anxiety—we discover that they begin to ease naturally on their own rather than intensify.

It feels completely unnatural to soften in the face of fear and anxiety and not resist the uncomfortable feelings and sensations that go along with these charged emotions. Yet this is the very thing we need to do to neutralize and transform the energy of fear and anxiety. As soon as we begin to feel the uncomfortable and unpleasant feelings and body sensations associated with fear and anxiety, the challenge is to try to relax and let go of resistance, allowing and giving full permission for these feelings and sensations to arise. We need to calmly say to ourselves something like: *I know these feelings and sensations are unpleasant, and I prefer not to have them, but it's okay they are with me right now. I know they won't actually hurt me, they are simply uncomfortable.*

Relaxing our resistance and guardedness in the midst of experiencing fear and anxiety gives our bodies and minds a powerful message that we are not in danger and no alarm bells need to be pressed. Responding in this way tends to have a pretty immediate calming effect. It allows us to step back from our conditioned responses and makes us less reactive to our fear and anxiety, which then helps to tone down the power and intensity of these feelings and sensations.

Allowing and accepting these uncomfortable feelings and body sensations rather than trying to run from, control, or eradicate these emotions has a paradoxical effect. It teaches us that we need not be afraid of our inner experience, and that our fear and anxiety is not the enemy, even if they make us feel uncomfortable. We learn that we can handle these unpleasant feelings and body sensations and we don't have to anticipate them with dread or feel helpless and out of control when they arise.

Once we allow and accept our fear and anxiety, it is helpful to "ventilate" the feelings and sensations by imagining putting lots of space around them. When we loosen our tight grip around these feelings and sensations, and create an airy and open feeling of spaciousness around our fear and anxiety, the energy of these emotions tends to lighten and dissipate. It is by creating a more conscious, permissive, and softer response to our fear and anxiety that these emotions and sensations naturally ease and transform into something that feels far more benign.

Beyond learning to bear uncomfortable feelings and sensations is learning to befriend them. This is a huge stretch for most of us, given how deeply unpleasant and unnerving these experiences can be. It helps to think of fear and anxiety as part of the self-protective hardwiring that dates back eons ago. Our nervous system is only doing what it is set up to do to try to keep us safe when we perceive threat or danger. Imagine smiling and speaking with your fear and anxiety, saying something like: *Hello there, fear and anxiety. Thanks for trying to look out for me. I know you have my best interest in mind. I appreciate you trying to keep me safe, though you can relax and not be so concerned about me as I have some other ways that I can take care of myself in this situation.* You may be surprised to see how these feelings and sensations ease more quickly when you welcome and befriend them rather than resist, reject, and try to run from them.

Guiding Intention: I practice letting go of resistance to fear and anxiety and allow and accept whatever feelings and sensations arise within me.

Affirmative Thought: I allow and accept any fear and anxiety when I am speaking (or performing), and I relax and soften toward these feelings.

Practice: Take a moment to close your eyes and vividly imagine yourself facing a speaking or performing situation that raises much fear and anxiety in you. Once you experience these feelings (to whatever degree you can create at this moment) begin to strongly resist the feelings and harden yourself against them, with a feeling of trying to fight them off or flee from them. Notice what happens when you resist your inner experience and try to conquer or control what is happening inside of you.

Now, take a deep breath and shake your body a bit to let go of that experience. Again vividly imagine the speaking or performing situation that raises a lot of fear and anxiety within you. This time, once you start to feel the fear and anxiety, try a very different approach. This time allow, accept, and give permission and space to what is happening within you. Imagine creating a relaxed, soft, and gentle approach toward your feelings and body sensations, letting go of resistance and compassionately responding to your inner experience. Notice the effect this has on your experience of these uncomfortable emotions and body sensations. For some people the effects are immediate and very noticeable. For others they happen more slowly and subtly. Either way, you will see the intensity of your fear and anxiety ease as you continue to use this approach whenever you face speaking or performing challenges.

CHAPTER EIGHT

Understanding the Emotional Brain

IT IS EASY TO FEEL FRUSTRATED BY HOW PERSISTENT AND UNRELENTING our fear and anxiety reactions are in the face of public speaking or performing challenges. Our panicky feelings and distressing body sensations seem to take on a life of their own, and they do not readily respond to our attempts to think rationally. While you may feel very alone with these intense reactions and wonder if something is wrong with you, take heart—this experience is not unique to you, and does not suggest that you are lacking in some way. Rather, it is characteristic of the way intense emotions and bodily sensations can get strongly conditioned in our nervous system. These feelings and sensations are generated by a series of biological processes that are not within your immediate, direct control. What is in your control, however, is how you respond to these feelings and sensations when they arise, and there is much you can do to influence the direction they take and their intensity and duration.

In his book *The Emotional Brain*, Joseph LeDoux describes the complex mechanisms by which the brain generates an emotional and physiological fear response. The brain is hardwired to quickly create emotional meanings of the stimuli it is experiencing, and much of this happens below the level of conscious awareness and separate from the part of the brain responsible for rational thought. As LeDoux states, "Emotional responses are, for the most part, generated unconsciously" and "once the fear system is turned on, it's hard to turn off—this is the nature of anxiety."

The main center for this fear response is a small region of the forebrain known as the amygdala. Once the amygdala detects a potentially threatening emotional stimulus it activates the autonomic nervous system, which then stimulates the adrenal glands to release adrenaline into the bloodstream. The release of adrenaline during highly stressful times affects a part of the brain called the hippocampus, a process that can strengthen memories of "trigger events," events that felt overwhelming or traumatic. Whenever situations, thoughts, or images that trigger the memory of such an event are encountered, the same fear response is reactivated—which means that response has become "conditioned." This often takes place on an unconscious level.

LeDoux notes that "Not only is fear conditioning quick, it is also very long lasting. In fact, there is little forgetting when it comes to conditioned fear." The good news, according to LeDoux, is that we can modify these conditioned responses by helping the higher, more advanced cortical areas of our brain override the conditioned response coming from the amygdala, which is the more primitive part of the brain.

Clearly, we are not at fault when the hardwiring of our brain activates a cascade of biochemical processes that lead to a conditioned fear response and ultimately sends us into a fight or flight fear reaction. The more primitive part of our brain is simply trying to protect us from danger, and the center where fear responses are generated is not capable of thinking rationally about all of this. While our biological hardwiring (which is also affected by our genetic makeup and environmental influences in our background) sets the stage for this conditioned fear response, it is important not to conclude that we are therefore helpless and can do nothing to influence our brain's functioning. In fact, the brain has a phenomenal capacity to adapt and change and is very influenced by how we interface with it.

You can influence how your brain and nervous system respond to an anxiety-triggering event by consciously engaging the body, mind, and spirit in ways that override the conditioned fear response. Throughout this book I present many ways to do this. The conditioned responses in the brain and nervous system don't usually change very readily or easily, so it is important to regularly review and practice the skills you are learning to imprint new pathways of responding. There may be moments when you temporarily lapse into old, conditioned patterns of thought, feelings, and behavior, so practice patience with yourself as you work on creating more conscious, skillful responses when your fear gets triggered.

Guiding Intention: I consciously choose how I respond whenever fear and anxiety arise within me, and I am able to influence the direction of my fear response.

Affirmative Thought: I consciously direct the focus of my thoughts to access the higher, rational part of my brain whenever I face a speaking (or performing) challenge.

Practice: Choose a time and space when you will not be disturbed. Begin by doing some deep breathing and grounding work to create a feeling of safety and support within yourself. Return to this feeling whenever you feel the need.

Next, think back to past speaking or performing events that have created anxiety and fear for you, or future situations that you will be facing. Start with the least anxiety-provoking images associated with those events. As you develop skill with this exercise you can move on to the more frightening.

Bring these associations and images to mind as vividly as possible to allow yourself to recreate the fearful feelings and the uncomfortable body sensations that you experience when facing the actual situations (or thinking about them in anticipation), even if they are less intense than when you are actually in the situation itself. Allow yourself to fully experience your feelings and body sensations, paying close attention to the conditioned fear response in your body and mind. Remind yourself that this fear response is part of the hardwiring of your brain and nervous system in their attempts to keep you safe, and it will not harm you.

See if you can step back from this conditioned fear response, and try to access the higher-level cortical part of your brain, which allows you to think clearly and rationally. Imagine strengthening the neuropathway to this part of your brain any time this fear response is reactivated.

Consciously focus on thoughts and images that support a rational and adaptive response to the situation you fear. One way to do this is to imagine someone you know who feels comfortable and at ease with speaking or performing and how his or her brain and thought process might respond to this situation. Anytime your fear gets activated, see if you can quickly shift your attention and access this higher-level brain functioning. Every time you do this, it strengthens your ability to engage the rational thought process and override your conditioned fear response when you face a speaking or performing challenge.

CHAPTER NINE

Helping Your Body Heal from the Trauma of Intense Fear

ONE PARTICULARLY SEVERE TYPE OF FEAR RESPONSE—ONE THAT can have powerful and far-reaching effects within the body and mind—is trauma, which occurs in response to facing a life situation that completely overwhelms one's coping capacities. Peter Levine, in his book *Waking the Tiger*, describes how the body and mind react profoundly to the experience of trauma and how its effects can become fixated within the person.

Levine believes that in trauma the "freezing" or "immobility" response is even more critical than the fight or flight response. He uses the analogy of what might happen in your car if you push down the accelerator and jam on the brake at the same time: "The difference between the inner racing of the nervous system (engine) and the outer immobility (brake) of the body creates a forceful turbulence inside the body similar to a tornado. This tornado of energy is the focal point out of which form the symptoms of traumatic stress." He further states, "Words can't accurately convey the anguish that a trauma-tized person experiences. It has an intensity that defies description."

The frozen residue of fearful energy persists in the nervous system and often shows up as post-traumatic symptoms whenever the person faces anything that resembles the original traumatic situation. The good news is that Levine believes we have an innate capacity to heal trauma, though it generally doesn't resolve on its own. We have to take conscious, active steps to transform and heal it.

Levine works with trauma primarily through what he calls the "felt sense," which refers to the direct experience of internal body sensations that reflect the symptoms of trauma and underlie the person's emotional reactions. The idea is to create a safe setting where you can allow yourself to fully experience your body's shifting internal sensations as it revisits associations to the earlier trauma. You become the observer of your body's internal responses as you allow the residue of fearful energy stored in the body to move through you. It is important to experience and observe the ebb and flow of your body sensations without judging, interpreting, reacting to, or trying to control them. In Levine's experience, this is what creates the conditions for healing and transforming the residue of trauma that is stored in the body.

Levine also believes that deep and intense fear responses are embedded in a more primitive, instinctual part of our brain referred to as the "reptilian brain." He says that "sensation is the language of the reptilian brain" and that working with the body sensations that are generated from this part of the brain are "the key to unlocking the mystery of trauma."

Most of the clients I work with have experienced public speaking or performing in a way that feels traumatic to them. This was the case for me too, years ago. Many of us can clearly remember the overwhelming experience of feeling intensely threatened and unsafe while speaking or performing—facing the threat of feeling trapped in a situation we cannot easily exit and the possibility of public humiliation. We experienced a disarming loss of control of our inner world—something that is not easily forgotten, on a conscious or unconscious level. The body stores the memory of this first experience of overwhelm and loss of control. Whenever we face a situation that has some association to the original traumatic event, the whole biochemical response is reactivated, including a flood of stress hormones, in a post-traumatic stress response.

The natural reaction to a post-traumatic stress response is to become even more frightened—even retraumatized—by the body's intense arousal and the accompanying feelings of helplessness and vulnerability. We assess this arousal as dangerous and end up frightened by our own thoughts, images, feelings, and body sensations, which lead to feelings of intense fear and loss of control. When the feelings and body sensations are at their strongest, it feels like you are spinning out of control and your internal state is heading rapidly down a steep and treacherous slope.

According to Levine, to resolve the underlying traumatic memory we must allow the energy of our intense body sensations to move through us and be released rather than try to control and suppress this energy. I am clearly not suggesting that you do the deep work of healing a post-traumatic response in the midst of a speaking or performing event! Rather, you may want to spend time on your own, or with a professional who can guide you through this process, to allow the pent-up energy of traumatic stress and fear in your body to naturally express itself and be released. This process typically is not done in just one sitting and requires patience and persistence as you move toward healing and transformation. Yet by facing your fear in this way—allowing it full expression within you while neutrally observing your body sensations—you are undoing the post-traumatic response to the original traumatic memory stored in your body and learning to not be afraid of the feelings and sensations that connect to this earlier trauma.

Guiding Intention: I work on healing and transforming any trauma associated with my fear of public speaking (or performing).

Affirmative Thought: I am able to handle any feelings or sensations that arise when I am speaking (or performing).

Practice: Do this exercise with a professional or trusted friend if it feels too overwhelming to do on your own. Also be sure to stop the practice session at any time you wish to do so.

Choose a time and space when you will not be disturbed. Begin by doing some deep breathing and grounding work to create a feeling of safety and support within yourself. Return to this feeling whenever you feel the need.

Think about past speaking or performing situations when you experienced feelings of overwhelm or that you associate with feeling trapped, helpless, or out of control. You may also want to think about future events you are anxiously anticipating.

Now float back in time and try to vividly recall the very first experience of feeling so deeply frightened and vulnerable in the face of a speaking or performing event. Bring these memories to mind with as much detail as possible and allow yourself to experience any feelings that may arise. Fully experience and neutrally observe your body sensations without reacting to what is going on in your body. Remind yourself that this fear response is simply an activation of stored body memories of an earlier feeling of trauma and that these feelings and sensations will not harm you.

Some of the body sensations may be quite intense while others may be more subtle. Some areas of the body may feel strongly aroused by the fear, and other areas may be less affected or not affected at all. Simply pay attention and quietly note to yourself (or a trusted other) what you observe. Pay attention to your breath patterns, your heartbeat, any muscle tightness or constriction, feelings of shakiness, heaviness or lightness, temperature changes, or any other body sensations.

Notice how these sensations naturally shift and transform as you simply watch them, without judgment or reactivity and without attempting to change them or control them. Learning to be with your fearful feelings and body sensations will support you in not being afraid of them when they do arise and will help to further heal and transform any traumatic memory that may be stored in your body.

CHAPTER TEN

Encouraging Your Brain
to Evolve

IT TURNS OUT THAT WE CAN TEACH OUR BRAIN TO EVOLVE. We can help it become more adaptive and resilient in handling challenging and stressful life circumstances, in addition to enhancing our overall personal growth and development. Research shows that, over time, the brain can actually be trained to create new neural pathways that allow our nervous system to respond in a calmer and more relaxed way when stressful situations arise, as well as develop higher levels of conscious awareness.

This is no "quick fix," of course, as our brain has been operating in certain habitual ways for many, many years, and it takes time and focus to retrain it to adopt different response patterns. While retraining your brain requires patience and persistence, it is exciting to know you do not have to be held hostage by your brain in times of stress and you can actually have some influence and control in helping your brain to evolve so that it becomes more resourceful and adaptive.

One helpful book on this topic is *Thresholds of the Mind* by Bill Harris. Harris explains that the brain generates four basic wave patterns of varying frequencies—alpha, beta, theta, and delta—which correlate with different states of mind. The beta pattern is the fastest (13–100+ Hertz) and is associated with normal waking consciousness, occurring when we are in a state of alertness, arousal, and concentration. While the brain creates some combination of the four categories of brain wave patterns much of the time, for most people beta waves are the most prominent in day-to-day life. While the lower-end beta waves allow us to be focused and productive, the higher-end beta waves (above 30 Hertz) tend to be associated with inner states of distress and anxiety. Strong feelings of separateness and the inner experience of a fight or flight response are common at the extreme high end of the beta wave range. This may give you some idea of what goes on in your brain when you are facing public speaking or performing challenges!

The alpha brain wave pattern operates at a somewhat slower frequency (8–12.9 Hertz) and becomes more prominent soon after we begin to relax—and is enhanced when our eyes are closed. While the brain is creating more alpha wave patterns, the body is producing calming neurochemicals as it moves into a relaxation response. The higher end of the alpha wave range is associated with a very receptive state of learning, while the lower-end alpha frequencies are associated with deeply meditative states. If a person has learned to create more alpha waves, his or her brain is more likely to respond to high stress in a calm, adaptive way rather than be pulled into a fight or flight reaction.

The theta brain wave pattern is slower still in frequency (4–7.9 Hertz) and happens when we are in a state of dreaming sleep associated with rapid eye movement. It is believed by some to be "the doorway to the unconscious mind" and is associated with enhanced understanding, insight, and integrative experiences, as well as increased creativity, memory, and inner healing. The most advanced meditators are often able to generate theta waves, though for only brief moments at a time.

The delta brain wave has the slowest frequency of all (0.1–3.9 Hertz) and happens most notably when we are in a state of dreamless sleep. This brain wave pattern is associated with feelings of oneness with others and with all life, in stark contrast to the feelings of separation and disconnection characteristic of high-end beta waves.

Another feature of the brain is called brain lateralization, meaning that one hemisphere of the brain is generally dominant over the other. The greater the brain lateralization, the more a person experiences feelings of separation, fear, stress, and anxiety.

The more a person can create the slower alpha, theta, and delta waves, the more communication occurs between the two hemispheres of the brain. This reduces feelings of separation and stress and enhances feelings of connection and balance. The belief is that a more balanced, synchronized brain raises the threshold of stress the person is able to handle and makes the person more immune to stress-related reactions.

Remarkably, the brain is naturally primed to evolve to a higher level of organization when prompted by situations that push us beyond our current coping capacity. This reminds me of a phrase popular in some personal development workshops: "Breakdowns precede breakthroughs." When we are in a state of "breakdown" there is generally a feeling of inner chaos, overwhelm, and confusion at these times as the threshold of our coping capacity is being reached. The interesting thing is that as our current ways of responding to the world are challenged, our brain is actually ready to restructure at a higher level, if only we can trust the process and not obstruct our brain's attempt to evolve.

Unfortunately, most people strongly resist this natural process of evolution, becoming frightened by the feelings of overwhelm, confusion, and loss of control that accompany it, and instead seek out the safety of their "comfort zone." The key to helping your brain evolve is to let go of trying to maintain tight control of your inner world as you move through the chaos, trusting that your brain is reorganizing and that your threshold for managing stressful life circumstances is increasing as you move through this process. This takes a huge leap of faith, as our sense of safety and security is often rooted in our experiences of predictability and control. Ironically, as we seek out our comfort zone and try to hold on tightly to creating predictability and control in our lives, we are limiting the growth and development of our brain.

So, the question becomes: How can you help your brain to grow and evolve—how can you cultivate a brain that operates more adaptively, especially when under stress—when fear and chaos threaten to overwhelm your inner world?

Among the many ways to help the brain evolve, one that has been researched and written about extensively is meditation. The benefits of meditation are many. In the context of this discussion, two of the most compelling are: meditation trains the brain to produce slower, more relaxed brain wave patterns, and meditation encourages balance and synchronicity between the two brain hemispheres. A regular meditation practice also helps a person cultivate higher levels of conscious awareness and reduces tendencies toward emotional reactivity, leading to a greater capacity to cope with stressful situations. The power of a meditation practice was noted in a January 2006 *Time* magazine article about the brain, which stated: "Scientists find that meditation not only reduces stress but also reshapes the brain."

I am an ardent believer in the power of meditation to evolve the brain and train the mind to better adapt to stress, as well as enhance overall personal growth. I have practiced meditation for many years, and I have seen some remarkable changes in my life, especially in the areas of reducing my emotional reactivity, increasing my level of conscious awareness and living less of the time on "auto pilot," and generally feeling calmer and more relaxed. My meditation practice has significantly improved the quality of my life and has allowed me to develop a deeper understanding and connection with myself and others.

Meditation is a powerful practice and it is well worth the investment of your time. To reap the greatest benefits it has to offer, you need to do it on a regular basis—ideally daily. Many people feel they do not have the time or patience to meditate, as their days are filled with much to do and their minds seem too busy to quiet down. If you find yourself resistant to taking time to meditate, consider starting with just five minutes of "quiet time" a day and see if you can build from there. Once you experience the value of this practice you will feel more inclined to learn more about meditation and will gladly extend your practice to at least fifteen to twenty minutes per day.

Many people give up meditation prematurely, as their minds seem too busy or they become bored or distracted. Please do not let a busy or bored mind stop you from staying the course with meditation, as your brain will benefit from this practice even if it seems challenging when you start out. We will be reviewing more about meditation in section two. If you are not currently meditating and experiencing the many benefits it has to offer, hopefully these discussions will inspire you to give meditation a try.

Guiding Intention: I trust in my brain's capacity to grow and evolve and develop an increased capacity to handle challenging and stressful situations.

Affirmative Thought: My brain is here to support me and is ready to reorganize at higher levels as I step up to meet my speaking (or) performing challenges.

Practice: Choose a time and space when you will not be disturbed. Settle into a comfortable seated position in which your body is relaxed but alert. Focus on your breath, simply watching the in-breath and the out-breath without trying to control them in any way. As you watch the breath you may want to make a mental note, saying silently to yourself, "breathing in," "breathing out," or you might create a count with each cycle of breath, moving from one up to ten, then starting at the count of one again with the next breath cycle.

When thoughts come to mind, as they inevitably will, simply observe that you are thinking and make a mental note, "thinking," without resisting the thoughts or chasing after them and embellishing upon them. Practice letting go of the thoughts as they arise in your mind and returning your focus to your in-breath and out-breath.

This may feel tedious and you may feel impatient or bored, as many people do initially. Or your mind may be racing with many thoughts. Sit with any uncomfortable thoughts, feelings, and sensations that come and simply observe and mentally note them in a neutral, nonreactive way (e.g., "impatience," "boredom," "busy mind") and return your focus to your breathing or to being in the present moment. Do this for five to ten minutes to start, and see if you can increase the time as you go along. Meditate daily if you can, as the benefits are cumulative. And be patient—it takes time to see the powerful effects that meditation can bring to your life.

Give meditation a fair try before deciding if it works for you or not. And note that there are many ways to go about meditation. This practice exercise is just a basic way to begin. If you want to learn more, I invite you to do some further reading or perhaps sign up for a workshop or retreat where you will be guided in developing a meditation practice that works best for you.

MIND

CHAPTER ELEVEN

Creating a Positive Attitude and a Willing Spirit

MOST OF US WOULD PROBABLY ADMIT THAT WHEN IT COMES to public speaking or performing we have a pretty bad attitude. Even if we are generally positive in other areas of our lives, it takes only the thought or mention of a presentation or performance to pull us into a negative state of mind. And, if we are often pessimistic in other areas of our lives, it pulls us down even further into that deep, dark hole. It is no surprise, then, that we often dread public speaking or performing. Our negative attitude gets layered on top of whatever anxiousness we already have about it and serves to intensify our feelings of gloom anytime we are called upon to speak or perform.

While it is understandable that we have fallen into some bad habits with our attitude toward speaking or performing, given how incredibly difficult this area of our lives has been for us, it is essential to consciously work on creating a more positive, optimistic attitude toward this challenge. Our attitude creates our general outlook and approach toward aspects of life and has a powerful influence over our thoughts, feelings, and behaviors. Consciously shaping our attitude and training our mind to have a more positive and optimistic out-look—even when we don't feel that way in the moment—is a key component in learning to approach speaking or performing in a more resourceful way. We can't afford to indulge in a negative, pessimistic mindset, as it takes our power away in an instant and leaves us feeling discouraged and defeated.

When we have a highly negative attitude toward anything in life, we im-mediately want to pull away and avoid whatever it is at any cost. We end up feeling forced to do something against our will if we can't get out of doing it, and we feel trapped if we can't exit the situation once we are in it. This leads us to experience a deep loss of control and creates a childlike feeling of helplessness, as if some higher authority is making us do something we don't want to do. These perceptions set off a cascade of distressing thoughts and feelings, and the intense negativity we experience is projected onto the external situation, making it appear overwhelmingly dreadful.

While it certainly is not easy to create a positive attitude toward anything that we fear intensely or anything that feels so overwhelmingly unpleasant, it is something we must consciously decide to adopt and practice as a way of breaking the vicious cycle that we repeatedly get caught in. Even when we don't feel that way, we can always *act as if* we have a positive and optimistic mindset as a way of beginning to move our attitude in the right direction.

One way to cultivate a positive attitude is to create the feeling of being a willing spirit, which suggests that you are open and willing to step forward even if something is not easy or pleasant for you. When you create a willing spirit with respect to speaking or performing challenges, you relax your strong resistance to these activities, which provides an opening for developing a better attitude toward it.

As you let go of resistance you regain a measure of control over your inner life, for you are consciously choosing to step up to the challenge, thereby removing yourself from the dynamic of feeling forced, controlled, or trapped by an external source. This shift opens the possibility for creating a more positive attitude as you work with your circumstances rather than fight against them. As you start to loosen the hold of negativity and resistance, you create a more open, flexible, and adaptive mindset, which allows you to view the situation more positively and optimistically.

Interestingly, research has been done on the biological correlates to attitudes of optimism versus pessimism when facing stressful circumstances, specifically involving the adrenal glands, which are the glands that release stress hormones. It turns out that when the mind perceives threat or danger—and is responding with a more pessimistic attitude—the adrenal cortex (the outer layer of the adrenal glands) starts to produce the stress hormone cortisol, which leads the nervous system into the classic fight or flight reaction, with elevated heart rate and respiratory rate and an increase in blood pressure. The more we focus on what could go wrong, the more cortisol is produced, leading to the often overwhelming and disorganizing effects of a strong output of this stress hormone.

On the other hand, people who hold a more positive, optimistic attitude and relate to a stressful event as a challenge and opportunity have a different hormonal response. The adrenal medulla (the adrenal core) is stimulated to release catecholamines, including epinephrines and norepinephrines. These hormones lead to a more excited, empowered and sometimes even euphoric feeling with increased mental clarity.

Given that our mind and body are so interconnected, it is vital that we consciously and deliberately guide our mind to release feelings of negativity and pessimism. Instead, we want to actively encourage an optimistic attitude and a willing spirit that will help support a healthy state of mind whenever we face speaking or performing challenges, as well as other challenging and stressful life situations.

Guiding Intention: I consciously adopt a more positive, optimistic attitude whenever I face speaking (or performing) challenges.

Affirmative Thought: I approach all speaking (or performing) challenges with a positive attitude and a willing spirit.

Practice: Write down a few statements that describe your attitude toward public speaking or performing. Be rigorously honest with yourself, noting ways in which you may feel and express a negative, pessimistic attitude. Close your eyes and take a moment to feel the impact of holding this attitude on your mind, body, and spirit. Then put a big X over this list and rip it up, bit by bit, to represent that the days of holding such a negative attitude are over and it is time for you to take charge of your attitude and move it in the direction you want it to go.

Now make a new list on a separate sheet of paper or in your journal, creating statements that support the positive, optimistic attitude that you want to develop going forward. Read your new list aloud with deliberateness and positive intention. Close your eyes and take a moment to internalize what you have written, feeling the impact on your mind, body, and spirit of holding a more positive attitude (remember to *act as if*, if you don't genuinely feel positive and optimistic in this moment). Keep your new list handy and review it regularly (closing your eyes and taking a few moments to internalize it each time) so you continue to reinforce your new, optimistic outlook rather than letting your mind gravitate back to a negative attitude and thought patterns from the past.

Additionally, work on cultivating a willing spirit as you approach speaking or performing situations. Take a moment to close your eyes and first create the feeling of an unwilling spirit—feeling resistant, forced against your will, controlled by an outside source, and trapped in a situation you don't want to be in. Notice how this affects your state of mind, body, and spirit and the impact this has on your attitude. Then, let go of this feeling with a strong, forceful exhalation.

Now consciously and deliberately create the feeling of a willing spirit— feeling open, cooperative, generous, willing to step forward, and accepting of whatever is being asked of you. Notice the very different experience this creates in your mind, body, and spirit and the effect it has on your attitude. Practice consciously letting go of all resistance to speaking and performing situations and adopting a willing spirit as you move toward your challenges.

CHAPTER TWELVE

Creating a Positive and Powerful Focus of Attention

MOST OF US ARE PRETTY GOOD AT KNOWING HOW TO FEEL BAD when it comes to public speaking or performing. We can quickly and easily create all sorts of intense negative feelings—anxiety, worry, self-doubt, fear, panic, dread, terror, frustration, anger, disappointment, regret, and any other "bad" feeling you can think of! It has been said that you can only feel really stressed, anxious, and upset if your mind is focused on things that you don't want to happen and are afraid might happen.

It is easy to see how this applies to public speaking and performing fear. For instance, we may be afraid that our voices may quiver, that it may be hard to catch our breath and keep going, that our hands may shake, that our minds may go blank and we will lose our train of thought, that people may notice something is off with us, that we may embarrass ourselves, and so on. The more we focus our attention on the things we fear, and want desperately to avoid, the more afraid we become—and the more likely these things are to happen in response to the additional fear (a self-fulfilling prophecy). Even if the things we are afraid of don't actually come to pass, we end up feeling a frightening loss of control as we imagine the unwanted things that could happen. This further ignites our fear and self-doubt and reinforces the vicious cycle we are caught in.

One of the keys to better managing our inner state and becoming less anxious is to shift our focus off of the things that we fear and want to move away from—the things we don't want to happen—and consciously and deliberately put our focus on the things we want to create and move toward. That means to both think about what we want to happen and create internal images of what we want (ideally, creating positive emotion associated with these thoughts and images as well).

For instance, instead of focusing on hoping that our symptoms don't arise and that other people don't see how anxious we are, it is far better to consciously and intentionally think about, imagine, and create the positive feeling of a calm, relaxed, confident presence through which you are openly and joyfully connecting and sharing with your audience. When you focus your attention on what you want to create, you move yourself more and more in the direction you want to go. This does not guarantee you will be symptom-free, but it does tend to significantly lessen your symptoms and creates within you a more confident and empowered feeling, which leads you toward a more positive outcome.

In order to shift to a positive focus, we have to switch out of autopilot mode, where our mind is conditioned to pay lots of attention to the things we are afraid of in an effort to protect us. Our mind tends to fear unpredictability and will often fill the gap of not knowing how things will turn out with negative predictions to ready us for a potential bad outcome. While our mind tries to brace us for a worst case scenario just so we are not caught off guard, this ends up leading to much distress and suffering and does not truly protect us— in fact, this does us more harm than good.

While preparing for the worst makes sense in truly dire situations, it is clearly not adaptive to be bracing ourselves for a calamity each time we step up to speak or perform. This grossly distorts the reality of the situation by inflating the probability that bad things will happen and minimizing the probability that things will turn out just fine (which is clearly the more probable outcome, even when we feel much fear and self-doubt). Imagine you had to bet a big sum of money on the likely outcomes of your speaking or performing situations. Do you think you would continue to grossly distort the probabilities and project terrible outcomes? Or would you more likely see the truth that no matter how difficult or challenging these situations might be, they will somehow turn out okay and probabilities are strongly in your favor that there will be no disastrous outcomes?

Granted, shifting your attention to a positive focus will not feel easy or natural at first. Yet it is vital that you loosen the grip of a negative focus—and all of the thoughts, images, and feelings that go along with it—as that mindset powerfully fuels the conditioned fear response. Consciously shifting to a more positive focus of attention, even when it doesn't feel natural or true to how you are feeling in that moment, will begin to break the pattern of negativity and transform feelings of fear, anxiety, and self-doubt. Given that we tend to attract toward us feelings and experiences that are congruent with our attitudes, beliefs, and ways of thinking, we are more likely to draw toward us positive, empowering feelings, experiences, and outcomes when we consciously choose to create a positive and powerful focus of attention.

To counter your conditioned fear response, you need to become more aware of your focus of attention. When you catch yourself feeling anxious and imagining scary things, shift your attention to a more positive and powerful focus. If you find it difficult to be more positive in your thinking, then simply try to "inch your way over" to a more positive focus by being just a slight bit less negative and a slight bit more positive. Keep gradually shifting away from the negative and toward the positive until adopting a solidly positive focus becomes easier (I discuss further how to do this in the next chapter).

Your mind will likely want to gravitate back to its old, familiar ways, especially as holding on to what we are used to often seems like a safer bet. Stay the course and know that it takes tenacity to train your mind to create a more positive and powerful focus. While this may seem challenging, it is well worth the effort. By training your mind to move you in the direction in which you want to go, you are far more likely to experience positive feelings and positive outcomes along the way.

Guiding Intention: I shift my attention to a positive focus anytime I find myself feeling anxious and afraid.

Affirmative Thought: I choose a positive and powerful focus of attention as I approach a speaking (or performing) challenge.

Practice: Become aware of the patterns of thoughts and images you create in your mind when feeling fear, anxiety, worry, and self-doubt related to public speaking or performing. Note the strongly negative focus in these thoughts and images and how they are focused on what you are afraid of, worried about, and don't want to happen. Note how these thoughts and images feed on themselves and reinforce your feeling worse and worse the more you hold this negative focus.

Now, let this focus go and consciously and deliberately shift your attention and create a positive focus in your thoughts, mental imagery, and emotion as you think about public speaking or performing. *Act as if* you had a more positive and powerful focus even if you don't genuinely think and feel this way at the moment (which is highly likely!). If you find yourself deeply entrenched in a negative mindset, you can also try to "inch your way over" to a more positive focus by trying to be just a slight bit less negative and a slight bit more positive and building upon this shift.

Think about and create an image of the experience and outcome you want, and imagine your mind paving the way in leading you in the direction you want to go. Create positive feeling states that are congruent with these positive thoughts and images, even if this doesn't come easily or naturally at first. Whenever your mind gravitates back to its old, familiar ways, become conscious of this as soon as possible (a cue would be anytime you start to feel bad again) and redirect your mind over and over toward a positive focus.

Work consciously to create a positive focus not only in situations of public speaking or performing but also in any other life situations that generate negative thoughts, images, and feelings. Your mind will become even better at creating a positive and powerful focus of attention the more you practice this skill in all areas of life.

CHAPTER THIRTEEN

Reaching for
Better-Feeling Thoughts

WE CAN EASILY GET CAUGHT IN A CYCLE OF NEGATIVE THINKING, often without realizing it. One negative thought builds upon another and before we know it, we are mired in negative feelings and our mood plummets rapidly. When we are in this negative mindset, we often feel mentally and emotionally drained, and we begin to notice a drop in our energy level and vitality.

Research has discovered that our thoughts have neurochemical correlates in the brain and nervous system, so we actually undermine our optimal functioning when we engage in negative thinking. On the flip side, the good news is that we can support healthy brain and nervous system functioning when we consciously and deliberately create positive thought patterns.

I have found the work of Esther and Jerry Hicks helpful in learning how to consciously create a more positive thought process and mood state—what they call reaching for "thoughts of relief" or "better-feeling thoughts." (Esther Hicks communicates words of wisdom by channeling spiritually guided information from an entity known as "Abraham." You can find out more about their work by visiting **www.abraham-hicks.com.**) They also speak of downstream versus up-stream thinking. Down-stream thinking reflects "going with the flow" and thinking in ways that support an effortless ease with life. It leads to a more relaxed, positive outlook and a thought process that uplifts the mood and spirit. Up-stream thinking, by contrast, reflects "swimming against the current" of life and expending much effort as we resist *what is* by focusing on what we perceive is wrong and what we don't like about our circumstances.

This type of thinking fuels states of stress and often creates darkness and heaviness in our mood and spirit.

When things are not going the way you would like them to, notice if you are engaged in up-stream thinking. If you are, the most important thing is to stop going against the current and redirect your focus to reaching for better-feeling thoughts—thoughts that bring relief from the way you are thinking about your circumstance. This is not to suggest that you should all of a sudden think really positive thoughts that do not feel genuine to you and try to convince yourself to believe in them when your thinking is on the other side of the spectrum. Thoughts exist on a continuum that range from highly negative to highly positive. It is important that you start from wherever you are in the moment and contemplate a series of thoughts that help you to "inch your way" farther from a negative mindset and toward a more positive mindset.

The best way to improve your mood quickly is to reach for a better-feeling thought that feels true to where you stand now and brings you some relief from your current distress. It helps to reach for a thought that makes sense to you as it brings into view a more positive aspect of your circumstance. Once you have found one thought that is more positive—or a thought that is simply less negative than the thought where you started—you can reach from there to an even better-feeling thought, creating a momentum that helps to shift you into a more positive mindset and a better-feeling mood state. As you do this, you can often feel relief in your body as your energy starts to lighten and your spirit is uplifted by your changing perspective on the situation.

During this process, you also begin to release the struggle, tension, and distress associated with up-stream thinking, which is associated with resisting *what is*. As you release the struggle around resisting *what is*, and continue to reach for better-feeling thoughts, it then becomes easier and quite natural to move into down-stream thinking, which has a feeling of relaxation, lightness, and ease.

When asked to speak or perform, we often automatically engage in up-stream thinking, which quickly builds momentum and pulls us toward feelings of fear, worry, anxiety, dread, self-doubt, frustration, and helplessness. These thoughts and feelings impact our mood and attitude, and, often within moments, we are caught in a vicious cycle of negativity that grows stronger and stronger as we fuel it with more up-stream thoughts. Some examples of up-stream thinking are:

- *I can't believe I have to do this presentation (performance). I don't want to deal with this. I hate the way this makes me feel.*
- *Why do I have to have this problem? I wish I were like others who don't have to deal with this. If anyone really knew what I go through, they would think there is something really wrong with me. I hate the fact that I get so anxious about this and can't seem to control it.*
- *I feel so out of control of myself when my body reacts like this. I don't want anyone to see me having a meltdown. I'm sure they would think less of me and lose respect for me if they saw me like this. I wonder what I can do to get out of having to do this. I hate having this problem and having it run my life.*

It is best to stop the cycle of up-stream thinking as soon as you catch yourself starting to get caught in it and notice your feelings and mood taking a nosedive. Guide your mind to reach for a better-feeling thought that could bring relief and help you head down-stream toward feeling more comfort and ease. Fortunately, as with the negative cycle, once you start to engage in better-feeling thoughts, these too create a momentum—this time a positive momentum that moves you toward a more relaxed and empowered feeling state and a lighter and brighter mood. Down-stream thinking might go something like this:

- *I know speaking (performing) doesn't come easily to me, so I have to take a moment to catch my breath right now and try to think this through in a way that helps me to better deal with it. I know I tend to react strongly when I am asked to speak (perform), but I also know that my fear reaction makes it seem much worse than it really is.*
- *These feelings are really uncomfortable, but I know they won't hurt me and that they eventually do ease and pass, especially if I don't fuel them with more negative thoughts. It is hard to stay positive when I feel this way, but it is important that I use my skills and do the best I can to keep*

reaching for better-feeling thoughts. I know that what I focus on and think about and say to myself—which are things I can control when I feel this way—definitely have a strong effect on my feelings and what is happening in my body.

- *Actually, it is encouraging to know that the better I get at focusing my mind and reaching for better-feeling thoughts, the more I can shift how I feel. At least I am learning some ways to help myself with this challenge—that is a good start.*

As you can see, thinking in a down-stream way can uplift your mood and spirit, and as you create some positive momentum with this type of thinking, it gets easier to keep reaching for more and more better-feeling thoughts that bring further relief. In fact, the hardest part is recognizing that you are heading up-stream so you can stop the negative momentum that is starting to build as quickly as possible, as it is easier to contain the damage and put out a fire if you stop adding more fuel to it. Your mind will follow your lead, based on what you consciously direct it to focus on, though you have to be firm and persistent when the negative pull of up-stream thinking is strong. When you give your mind a clear and compelling directive to reach for better-feeling thoughts, it will ultimately comply and begin searching for things to think about that make you feel better about yourself and your circumstances.

Guiding Intention: I choose to focus my mind on down-stream thinking and reach for better-feeling thoughts that bring relief.

Affirmative Thought: I choose to think better-feeling thoughts that bring me feelings of relief whenever I am faced with a speaking (or performing) challenge.

Practice: Reflect upon the up-stream thinking you engage in when you are facing a speaking or performing challenge, and write a paragraph that captures the essence of your thought stream. You may find these thoughts overlap quite a bit with ones you came up with in the two prior exercises related to attitude and focus of attention. If so, write down your thoughts anyway to help further build awareness of negativity in your thought patterns. Title this page "Up-Stream Thinking" (you could also subtitle it "Thoughts That Make Me Feel Even Worse Than I Already Do!"). Try to write your exact thoughts (or what you imagine they might be if you are not conscious of them) so you can become more aware of how your mind works and how you get caught in this vicious cycle of negativity.

When you are finished, on a separate sheet of paper or in your journal write the title "Down-Stream Thinking" (or you could subtitle this "Reaching for Better-Feeling Thoughts That Bring Me Feelings of Relief!"). Start by considering thoughts that are less negative than your original thoughts and build momentum with increasingly better-feeling thoughts that feel true and believable to you. Write down as many as you can think of in a paragraph or two. If you get stuck and can't come up with many thoughts like this, imagine how someone else who has a more positive, optimistic mindset would think when facing a speaking or performing challenge.

After you complete this part of the exercise, I encourage you to put an X through the up-stream thoughts and rip up and dispose of the paper containing these thoughts. Regularly read and review your down-stream thoughts to help you internalize this method of reaching for better-feeling thoughts that bring relief.

When you are actually faced with a speaking or performing challenge, or any other life situation that is difficult or stressful for you, practice this method of looking for relief by reaching for better-feeling thoughts. The more you practice this type of thinking in day-to-day situations that cause you tension and stress, the more you will remember to think this way when the bigger life stressors come up. Pay attention to the differences in your attitude and mood and the feelings in your body when you are engaged in up-stream thinking versus down-stream thinking, and notice the power that comes from consciously redirecting your thoughts in a way that provides relief from distress.

CHAPTER FOURTEEN

Creating Resourceful Beliefs

WHAT WE BELIEVE ABOUT OURSELVES AND THE WORLD AROUND US has a powerful influence on our experience of life, yet because our beliefs tend to be unconscious we generally don't see the crucial role they play. The foundation of our belief system is created in our early life experiences and interactions with others, especially significant others who have a major impact on our beliefs. These experiences and interactions include not only the more blatant and dramatic events of our lives, but also the more subtle and less obvious experiences.

If we had life experiences early on that led us to feel unsafe, unprotected, uncared for, or not good enough, this colors our view of ourselves, others, and the world around us. As children, we do not have the maturity or cognitive skills to make sense of what is happening. We tend to personalize our negative experiences and make ourselves at fault or make gross generalizations about ourselves, others, and what is happening to us. We often carry these unconscious beliefs, unseen and unchallenged, into adulthood, where they become a filter for our subsequent life experiences.

Human beings tend to seek consistency between what they believe and what they experience in life. As a result, we unconsciously filter our life experiences by deleting, distorting, and generalizing what we perceive about ourselves, others, and our world so it is congruent with what we believe. We may unconsciously attract to ourselves people and situations that affirm our beliefs, or we may misperceive, misinterpret, or ignore that which does not fit into our belief system so our beliefs are left intact. The well-known phrase *self-fulfilling prophecy* speaks to the power of our beliefs as a driving force in shaping what happens to us in life, increasing the probability of either positive or negative outcomes depending upon what we believe.

Clearly, then, it is important that we become conscious of our hidden beliefs and the powerful role they play in shaping our perceptions and expectations. When we do, we are then able to have some choice in whether or not we will let them dictate the course of our lives.

It isn't easy to choose to believe something different, as most of our beliefs are deeply ingrained and reinforced over time and we tend to trust that they express basic, absolute truths about ourselves, others, and life. Even when we know rationally that a limiting belief may not serve us well, and may not even be true, we still tend to hold tightly to it because it has become such an integral part of our identity and our life view.

One way to loosen our attachment to our beliefs, especially those that do not serve us well, is to adopt what is called the *witness* or *observer* position. From this position we can take a step back from the mind and develop curiosity about the way it works, and be similarly curious, rather than reactive, about our feelings, perceptions, and interpretations of our life experiences. When we are having negative feelings, instead of further fueling our upset by reacting to our emotional state, we can step back and observe, becoming curious about what underlying core beliefs may be creating such distress within us. Instead of automatically believing in the truth of our beliefs and being unconsciously propelled by them, we are able to bring our beliefs into conscious awareness, take a closer look at them and consciously choose whether or not we will continue to believe in them.

While long-standing, limiting beliefs may not fall away in one fell swoop, the very act of stepping back and creating conscious awareness begins to loosen their hold on you. The more you continue to neutrally observe and be curious about what negative beliefs are driving your fear and other distressing emotions, the less you will automatically fall into the trap of believing in things about yourself, others, and the world around you that do not serve you, and are often untrue.

Bill Harris, who teaches about how the mind creates beliefs, states, "Since everything is true to the person who believes it, evaluating beliefs based on whether they are 'true' or 'false' is not helpful. Doing so is indulging in circular, fallacious logic. Conscious, happy people evaluate beliefs based on whether or not they are resourceful—in other words, on whether or not they create the desired results and experience of life. . . .What you believe determines a great deal of what happens to you. . . . So, if whatever you deeply believe will end up being true for you, why not believe what will give you the best experience, and the best outcome?" He goes on to say, "The main point here is that you can choose what you want to believe, and therefore experience the results of that belief in your life. You don't have to believe whatever seems true based on past experience" (from an online course taught by Bill Harris through Centerpointe Research Institute—visit **www.centerpointe.com** for more information).

Let me offer an example to illustrate these concepts. Let's say that you grew up in a way where you came to believe that being mentally and emotionally strong and in control is very important and that feelings of vulnerability are a sign of weakness and mean you are inadequate in some way. You also came to believe that it is important to please other people, gain their approval, and have them respect you. You further came to believe that you always have to do well and be held in high esteem by others in order to be a valuable person who has a sense of worth and belonging. Based on these beliefs, you set about making choices that led you down the path of high standards, high achievements, and feelings of confidence, strength, and control in your life.

Then, one day an unexpected event occurred such that, out of the blue, you felt a terrifying sense of loss of control while in the public eye as you were speaking or performing. Your core beliefs about what it means to lose control and for others to see you in such a vulnerable, frightened state kicked in very strongly. You interpreted this event as very shameful and humiliating and came to believe that others would lose respect for you. You also lost respect for yourself for not being as strong and "together" as you thought you were, or should be. You started to believe something is wrong with you and that you had better hide this from others, so they would not look down on you or think less of you.

You started to believe that speaking or performing is scary and unpredictable and that you couldn't trust yourself or the situation going forward. Based on this belief you started to avoid speaking or performing situations as much as possible and when you did have to speak or perform, you were strongly on guard for the possibility of this happening again. Those negative core beliefs created feelings of worry, apprehension, fear, anxiety, dread, self-doubt, terror, and shame and led to avoidance or highly guarded behaviors whenever you had to step up to speak or perform.

Taking this example a step further, let's assume you are becoming more conscious of your limiting beliefs by adopting the witness or observer position. You begin to become aware of the negative beliefs from your upbringing that don't serve you well and how you have carried those beliefs into your adult life. You notice how you have created highly negative interpretations and meanings concerning the speaking or performing events where you felt a frightening loss of control, and you see how this set in motion a chain reaction of thoughts, feelings, and behaviors that fueled the cycle of fear and strengthened its power.

You now consciously decide to adopt a different set of beliefs that better serve you. You create new interpretations and meanings about what happened, reworking your core beliefs so they support rather than undermine your trust and confidence in yourself related to public speaking or performing. Your new belief system also challenges the negative expectations you have created for future speaking or performing events and allows an opening for you to create positive expectations going forward.

You work on revising your view of past speaking or performing experiences and consciously choose a more positive and empowering belief system, perhaps using some of the following resourceful beliefs:

- *It's okay to feel vulnerable and afraid at times. This is part of being human—I am no different than others. It's not realistic to think that I will feel strong and in control all of the time.*
- *Everyone has areas of vulnerability, even if they look completely confident and in control on the outside.*
- *While I prefer people to appreciate what I have to offer, I don't need their*

acceptance and approval.

- *Sometimes unexpected things happen and people experience a loss of control. If this happens to me, the most important thing I can do is support myself fully and use my skills to regain my equilibrium.*
- *If I lose my composure I can quickly regain it again. I simply need to keep my mind focused on those things that help me reconnect with my inner stability and strength, and not focus attention on things that throw me off balance.*
- *I know I have strengths I can tap into. It's important that I stay focused on my strengths whenever I feel unsure of myself.*
- *I will approach this situation as a challenge and use it as an opportunity to practice my skills and build courage. I will step up to the situation even when I feel afraid, and I will get stronger in the process.*
- *I am responsible for the way I think about this, and I will do all I can to create a positive attitude and an empowered state of mind. When I do this, I am much more likely to experience a positive outcome.*
- *I can learn important lessons from any challenge I face in life, and I'm determined to learn all I can from this challenge to benefit me for my future.*

Imagine for a moment what it would be like to hold this set of beliefs that support and empower you. Imagine letting go of beliefs that rob you of your power and your belief in yourself, create barriers between you and others, and diminish your experience of life. Beliefs are not absolute truths. We get to choose what we believe in. We don't have to hold on to beliefs that do not serve us. Choose your beliefs consciously and wisely, as they have tremendous power to direct the course of your life.

Guiding Intention: I observe my beliefs and challenge those that do not serve me well.

Affirmative Thought: I consciously choose beliefs that allow me to create the experiences and outcomes I want with public speaking (or performing).

Practice: Take some quiet time to reflect upon your beliefs. Write down all of the limiting beliefs you hold about yourself, others, and the situation of public speaking or performing. You may want to reflect upon the time when this fear initially took hold so strongly and the beliefs you had about what was happening and what it meant about you and your life. You may also want to reflect on your early life experiences and the beliefs you formed back then that may have contributed to negative interpretations and meanings concerning your experiences with public speaking or performing.

Take on the role of a curious observer of yourself as you reflect on your belief system and write down whatever comes to mind, without editing or judging what you write. Deeply ingrained beliefs tend to reside in the unconscious mind, and it is important to allow these beliefs a safe space to surface so you can create more consciousness about them.

Once you have identified the negative beliefs that are fueling the fear, step back and imagine the impact they would have on anyone who held them. After you complete this part of the exercise, I encourage you to draw an X through these limiting beliefs and rip up and dispose of the paper containing them.

Now begin to challenge these beliefs. Consider resourceful beliefs you could consciously create going forward. Reflect on new interpretations of your past experiences with this fear. Write these new, positive beliefs down on a different sheet of paper or in your journal. Then, say each one aloud in a strong, bold voice, closing your eyes and breathing in deeply, and try to feel the deeper truth of each of these new beliefs (remember to *act as if* these new beliefs are true even if you don't quite feel that way yet). Continue to review these new beliefs regularly until they are more deeply internalized within you.

CHAPTER FIFTEEN

My Mind
Is My Ally

MOST OF US HAVE HEARD THE SAYING, *I AM MY OWN WORST ENEMY*. Unfortunately, this is a well-known expression because so many people can relate to it. Many people treat themselves in ways they would never think of treating those they most love and care about. They can be harsh, and even abusive at times, in the way they speak to themselves. One of my clients, for instance, recently acknowledged that he acts like a bully toward himself, condemning himself with self-berating thoughts when he experiences feelings of inadequacy and failure. Not only does he end up feeling bad about the initial upset that led him to feel like he is not measuring up, but the self-condemning treatment leaves him feeling even more diminished as a person and quite helpless and hopeless about his ability to succeed when faced with similar challenges in the future.

While others may not be so inwardly hostile, they may be generally un-supportive and lacking in kindness toward themselves, especially during their most difficult moments. They may feel frustrated and upset with themselves for feeling vulnerable and afraid. They feel they "shouldn't" be feeling this way, and they often have great difficulty treating themselves with understanding, acceptance, and compassion.

I often ask clients to reflect on how they would speak with their child, a dear friend, or anyone they love and care about who is feeling very anxious and afraid. They are quick to note that they would never say to their loved ones what they think and say to themselves. Instead, they are readily able to find words that are kind, compassionate, encouraging, affirming, and generally supportive when they think of a loved one struggling.

This is the blueprint we need to follow for how we treat ourselves, yet many people find it far more challenging to give this type of caring and support to themselves than to give it to others. Sometimes complete strangers (and even our pets) receive kinder treatment from us than we give to ourselves!

For many of us, our minds have fallen into some bad habits when it comes to facing difficult feelings and stressful circumstances. We unconsciously and reflexively react to those feelings and circumstances in ways that drive our distress deeper and magnify the situation we find ourselves in so it seems even worse than it is. We need to step back from these automatic, reactive patterns of the mind and, instead, consciously relate to our mind as an ally who will help us under all circumstances and at all times. With conscious attention to changing our thought patterns, we can cultivate a positive alliance with our mind and have it guide and support us rather than thwart and undermine us when we are dealing with a challenge.

A favorite expression that I regularly use is: *My mind is my ally.* It reminds me that my mind is there to support me if only I allow and encourage it to do so. I think of my relationship with my mind as a partnership, where my mind wants to help me out, as it is good for both of us when I am handling situations with less stress and more ease. Allowing and encouraging my mind to help me means I have to stop engaging in automatic, habitual patterns of reactivity and, instead, be open and willing to learn a better way of thinking about and responding to stressful situations. I am always amazed at how this shift in consciousness and focus opens up new possibilities for responding more supportively toward myself and more effectively with respect to the circumstance I find myself in.

So, how do we go about cultivating our mind as an ally? The first step is always increased awareness. Given that the mind's tendency to react in negative, habitual ways is generally driven by unconscious, conditioned reactions, we need to first become aware of our patterns of reactivity to stressful circumstances. To illustrate this, let's use an example that we can all relate to: finding out that we have to speak or perform, especially when it involves our most challenging type of speaking or performing situation.

Upon hearing the news, most of us have an automatic and deeply intense negative reaction in our mind and experience immediate feelings of dread and foreboding. (Those of us who have made progress in this area may find the intensity of the negative reactions far less, though a residue of some degree of reactivity may remain.) Our conditioned mind often reacts with a stream of negative and frightening thoughts and images that provoke a range of overwhelming and stressful feelings. As we react to these thoughts, images, and feelings, we unconsciously activate feelings of helplessness and loss of control. And the vicious cycle continues until we are so deeply caught in a loop of fear, anxiety, and self-doubt that we can see no way out and feel even more trapped and helpless.

This is a classic example of a strongly conditioned unconscious fear response. To shift this pattern of reactivity we must consciously step in and train our mind to be our ally. While our mind might continue to be pulled unconsciously toward the conditioned fear and negativity for some time, we need to focus our attention strongly on directing our mind toward more positive and empowering thoughts. We also need to guide our mind to think in ways that express kindness and support toward ourselves rather than turn against ourselves with frustration and upset when we are struggling.

To guide our mind to become our ally and direct it to focus more positively, we might use conscious and deliberate thought patterns such as these:

- *Okay, I know this is not easy for me, so let's first take a few nice, deep breaths and slow things down.*
- *It's most important right now that I take a step back and not react in those old ways, as that just adds to the fear even more.*
- *Let's consider some new ways to respond. How might someone whose mind is their ally think about a stressful situation like this?*
- *What are some things I can think about that are comforting, reassuring, and affirming about the situation?*
- *What are some things I can think about that remind me of my strengths and my ability to handle stressful situations in the past?*

- *If someone I love and care about deeply was facing a challenge like this, what would I say to them? Let me offer this same kind of support to myself.*
- *Let's focus on what I've learned about approaching these challenges more positively and consciously apply a few of these things right now.*
- *What's great is that each time I consciously change my conditioned patterns and choose a better approach, it's helping to create new, more positive pathways in my mind.*
- *My mind is my ally. I will continue to train my mind to support me at times of stress and pressure so that my mind and I work as partners, focusing on things that are positive and empowering to me.*

As you might imagine, consciously and deliberately guiding your mind in a more positive direction begins to release the hold of the automatic, negative, conditioned fear response, which frees your mind to develop new possibilities for responding more adaptively and skillfully. As you consciously relate to your mind as your ally, and begin to trust that it will support you, it becomes easier to work in partnership with your mind when you are under pressure and facing stressful circumstances.

Guiding Intention: I work in partnership with my mind as I consciously direct my thoughts to be more positive and supportive.

Affirmative Thought: My mind is my ally and is there to support me every time I am faced with a speaking (or performing) challenge.

Practice: Take some time to reflect upon how you speak to yourself when you are faced with a public speaking or performing challenge and are experiencing feelings of fear and vulnerability. Also reflect on how you speak to yourself after a speaking or performing event, especially if you are not pleased with how it went. Write this down on a sheet of paper so you become more aware of how you relate to yourself and treat yourself when faced with this type of stressful situation (some of your responses may overlap with those in other exercises in this section, though you may also come up with some different ones with each exercise).

Take particular notice of any tendency to be harsh and critical toward yourself for having this fear and how that creates even more distress within you. After you complete this part of the exercise, I encourage you to put an X through these unsupportive ways of responding to yourself and rip up and dispose of the paper, acknowledging that you are determined to find a better way to treat yourself when you are feeling vulnerable and afraid.

Now consider how your mind might think and what images it might create when it is working as your ally in the same circumstances. On a separate sheet of paper or in your journal write down a stream of thoughts and images that your mind might create when operating as your ally, both in anticipation of a future event and when you are about to step up to the challenge. Also consider how your mind might respond if you are not pleased with how things go in a speaking or performing event.

Have a chat with your mind. Let it know that you would like to create a partnership and have it work on your behalf when facing pressured or stressful situations, especially speaking or performing events. Continue to focus on training your mind to work for you rather than against you under all circumstances, especially the most difficult ones. Enjoy creating a new relationship with your mind and discovering the tremendous support it can offer.

CHAPTER SIXTEEN

Meditation
for the Mind

ONE OF THE BEST WAYS TO TRAIN THE MIND TO BE MORE RESOURCEFUL is by engaging in a regular meditation practice. Many people have never tried to meditate, thinking they don't have the time or patience to sit quietly, especially if it takes time away from getting things done. Others may resist meditation, feeling anxious at the thought of sitting down quietly with themselves without all of the external distractions that usually occupy their attention. Some people who have tried to meditate give up on it prematurely, thinking they are not good at it because their mind is so busy and they are unable to quiet their mind.

Many people have the mistaken idea that the goal of meditation is to "empty" the mind of thoughts and create a peaceful, blissful state. While this may happen for a few, especially for more advanced practitioners, most beginners of meditation experience a busy mind with many thoughts coming and going. This is sometimes called "the monkey mind" or "the puppy mind" to convey the high degree of mental activity people may experience when they attempt to sit quietly with their mind.

Actually, the purpose of meditation is not to clear the mind of all thoughts but to become aware of your thoughts and watch them come and go without getting caught up in your thought process. Meditation teaches us to observe our thoughts without identifying with or reacting to them. It also teaches us how to not get lost in thought or in the "stories" we create in our head as one thought leads to another and yet another. Meditation powerfully trains the mind to step back from habitual patterns of thinking and reactivity and encourages us to observe our inner process with curiosity in a nonjudgmental way. It supports the development of a deeper level of self-awareness and a higher level of consciousness in how we approach life.

A meditation practice provides an opportunity to learn to loosen our attachment to our thoughts and to notice how we construct our perception of reality with our thoughts. Much of our inner agitation and suffering comes from automatic thought patterns that operate unconsciously, outside of our awareness. Through meditation, we learn to step back from our thoughts and not be swept away by them. We learn to not believe in our thoughts as ultimate and absolute truth just because we happen to think them.

Another valuable aspect of meditation is learning how to calm the mind through consciously focusing our attention in the present moment. The mind often jumps from one thought to another and may start to race at times, especially when we feel anxious, which can further agitate the mind and body. We may be thinking about what has happened in the past or projecting thoughts into the future, and not be grounded in our present moment experience. Meditation teaches us to slow down and be more aware of the present moment (also referred to as mindfulness), which is a deeply relaxing and calming experience and often allows us to feel our aliveness more fully.

Many different types of meditation practices are available, and there is no one "right" way for everyone. Some people sit quietly and focus on their breath, watching the inhalation and exhalation over and over again and bringing their attention back to the breath whenever it wanders. Others focus on a simple word or phrase that helps them to relax and access a deeper awareness. Some people use a designated mantra for this purpose, though any word or phrase can work if it helps you to relax the mind and body and focus on the present moment. Others may use a series of meditative passages that encourages a more enlightened state of mind. And others may listen to guided meditation CDs as a way of directing their process.

I have practiced meditation in several different ways over the past few years and have gained enormous benefit from sustaining a regular practice. When I first started, I could hardly sit still for five minutes. I have always been a very active person, highly invested in getting things done. I found it hard to justify taking the time to sit and do nothing when I could be getting things accomplished. After hearing and reading about the benefits of meditation over and over, I finally decided it was worth trying, despite my strong resistance to devoting time to being still and not productive, in the usual sense of the word. I now see my meditation time as highly productive in training the inner workings of my mind for my higher good, and I deeply appreciate the benefits that this practice has brought to my life.

I made a commitment to myself to begin a daily practice and to start with very small steps. Once I finally got myself to sit down, I limited my time to five to ten minutes, short enough so I could bear the restless feelings that showed up as I watched my breath and tried to bring myself into the present moment. I called this my "quiet time," as it did not feel like I was doing a formal meditation practice. As I began to get a bit more comfortable with sitting quietly, I started to increase the time and eventually worked my way up to twenty to thirty minutes. I also went through a phase of listening to deeply relaxing music that helped me to focus my mind in the here and now.

After attending a retreat, I adopted a slightly different type of practice where I focused on four key phrases that helped to deepen and expand my consciousness. I would slowly rotate my focus on each of the phrases throughout a meditation session. They were:

- *Be in the present moment and focus on breath*
- *Relax deeply*
- *Let my mind be my ally*
- *Be open to possibilities*

Focusing on these four simple phrases helped to calm, settle, and expand my mind greatly. I often come back to these phrases at times of stress or to center myself before starting a busy day.

In recent years I also tried a different form of meditation in which I listened to a CD using audio headphones for thirty to sixty minutes. This program, called Holosync and developed by Bill Harris at Centerpointe Research

Institute, uses technology that embeds sound frequencies on the CD tracks that entrain the brain to go into alpha, theta, and delta wave frequencies. These slower wave patterns move the brain toward states of deeper relaxation and higher consciousness and have the potential to accelerate the pace of the brain developing these new neural pathways.

While this program can yield great benefit, it is not for everyone, as it requires a substantial investment of time. For those who are interested in meditating with sound technology such as this, I encourage you to look into it. Other, less time-intensive programs are also available; information can be found by doing some online research.

My message in sharing all of this is that beginning a daily meditation practice and making it a priority is well worth the investment of time. While some people choose to meditate on an occasional or as-needed basis, those who maintain a regular practice are more likely to gain the most benefit that meditation has to offer. Even if you practice just five to ten minutes a day, doing it on a daily basis helps you integrate its benefits more fully by inviting present moment awareness and a higher level of consciousness into your life each day. And by making it a regular, predictable part of your routine, you don't leave finding time to do it to chance.

I hope this discussion inspires you to consider starting a daily meditation practice and sustaining it over time. The benefits are cumulative and many. I encourage you to give it at least a month, if not three to six months, to see what it can do for you. For some, the shifts are subtle, while for others they are quite dramatic. Approach it with an open mind and no expectations. Rather, let it be a discovery process, seeing how your mind and body respond to slowing down and paying more attention to your inner life and your present moment experience.

After giving meditation a fair try, you can then decide for yourself if the benefits warrant the time invested. If you are not able to create a daily practice, make time for it as regularly as is possible for you. At the very least, I encourage you to take some quiet time in the day, or days, prior to a speaking or performing challenge to help relax and calm your mind. Quiet, meditative time can help settle and bring clarity to the mind, especially in those times when we need it most.

Guiding Intention: I open myself to the benefits of a meditation practice and make time for this in my life.

Affirmative Thought: I focus on being in the present moment and my mind settles and feels calmer when I face speaking (or performing) challenges.

Practice: I encourage you to consider creating a daily meditation practice (or whatever frequency seems possible for you) if you do not have one already in place. Start out in a way that feels best for you.

If you have never meditated before, you may want to start out with five to ten minutes and simply try to bring your attention to your breath and present moment awareness. You may choose to do this with relaxing music. You may also want to consider listening to a guided meditation CD (there are many to choose from, and you may have to try out a few before finding the one that works best for you). You may also want to read a book on meditation if you are interested in learning more about it. You can also look into the sound technology option to accompany your meditation practice and see if this feels right for you.

Whatever way you choose, I encourage you to give your practice a fair try over the next few months and set your expectations aside. Instead, adopt a "beginner's mind" perspective and be a curious observer, noticing any shifts that happen within you as you devote regular time and attention to cultivating a meditation practice.

You may also want to practice mindfulness during your daily activities by consciously moving your attention to present moment awareness at different moments throughout the day. Rather than being lost in thoughts about past and future, or labeling your present situation with judgments, you are invited, through mindfulness practice, into a full and direct experience of the present moment. You become aware of your breath and the aliveness within your body, as well as the full sensory experience of what is going on around you—the sights, smells, sounds, tastes, and the feel of your experience in the present moment. This practice brings you to another level of conscious awareness, where you are experiencing life more directly rather than as a reflection of your mind's projections.

You will see the greatest benefit from combining a meditation practice with practicing mindfulness in daily life. While it is best to do these practices on a regular basis, you may also choose to devote more time to them in the days or weeks prior to a speaking or performing challenge. This will help you disengage from mind chatter and create the conditions for establishing calm and clarity in your mind.

CHAPTER SEVENTEEN

Helping the Mind
to Let Go

MANY PEOPLE HAVE DIFFICULTY LETTING GO OF DISTRESSING thoughts and feelings. In fact, those thoughts and feelings seem to hold us hostage at times, and we cannot seem to get free of them no matter how hard we try. This is especially true for many of us who have issues with control and perfectionism. We tend to have set expectations about how things should be with ourselves, others, and the world around us and how our life experience should go. When things don't go as we expect, we often fight against the reality. We may react by creating upsetting stories in our heads about whatever is happening and then get lost in our stories, believing them to be true, forgetting that our minds have made them up and they don't represent objective reality or absolute truth.

We may try to distract ourselves from these upsetting thoughts and feelings or try to create a more positive way of thinking and feeling, but sometimes our inner distress returns and we find we can't easily shake it. At those times one useful tool to consider trying is the Sedona Method˚. This simple yet powerful system for guiding the process of letting go has been something I have found useful for myself and for many clients. Though simple, it can be profoundly freeing to the mind as it helps to release the mind's grip on whatever it is clinging to.

The basic method starts by welcoming whatever distress-causing thoughts, feelings, and reactions you are having. Our natural tendency is to push back from inner distress and to tense our mind and body as we fight against experiencing uncomfortable feelings. We usually try to quickly escape the inner discomfort through distraction or through attempts to immediately change what we are feeling. Rather than helping us to let go of our distress, these responses can end up amplifying our negative thoughts and feelings as we resist our inner experience.

Welcoming rather than running from our uncomfortable thoughts and feelings requires a shift in attitude and a willingness to let whatever is happening inside of us be okay, without judging it as "bad" or "wrong." We can let it be okay that we are not feeling very good or responding very well to whatever is happening. We don't have to judge ourselves for this or rush to rid ourselves of this unpleasant inner experience. Instead, we can allow our distress to be what it is and accept that it is okay to be exactly where we are in this moment.

Once we release our resistance and welcome our thoughts and feelings no matter how unpleasant they may be, we are usually able to relax a bit and let go of our inner struggle. Whatever tension we are feeling begins to ease, and we often feel the grip of our distressing thoughts and feelings loosening, which leaves us in a better position to further the process of letting go.

The Sedona Method offers an exercise to help you get a better idea of what the letting go process feels like: Start by tightly gripping something in your hand to the point of noticeable discomfort, then slowly open up your hand and loosen the grip a little, then open your hand a bit more, and finally release what you were holding completely and let it drop to the floor, noticing the freeing sensation that goes along with releasing whatever you have been gripping.

The next part of the method includes a set of three questions that you slowly and gently ask yourself, inviting yourself to move toward the possibility of letting go but never forcing the process or the timing. The three questions (reproduced by permission of Sedona Training Associates, **www.sedona.com**) are:

- *Could I let this go?* (reflecting a curiosity about whether letting this go is within the realm of possibility)
- *Would I let this go?* (reflecting a curiosity about your willingness to let it go, once it seems possible)
- *When?* (an invitation to let it go now, if that feels possible)

It helps to have an attitude of neutrality about this process and not have an agenda—for instance, thinking you have to let go of something quickly to be successful with this method. After all, we can't force or control the process of letting go. In fact, the more you try to force or control it, the less likely it is to happen. A very relaxed stance is the key, gently inviting yourself to release and let go and letting the outcome be whatever it is. You may find that cycling through these questions several times allows you to ease toward letting go gradually, always being willing to accept how the process naturally unfolds for you.

It is also perfectly acceptable if you truly do not feel willing, able, or ready to let something go—in this moment, or ever, for that matter. You would then work on letting that be okay, releasing and letting go of your need to change your reactions and any negative judgments you may have about them.

One other aspect of this method I want to briefly mention is the identification of three basic "wants"—the wish for approval, the wish for control, and the wish for safety and security. One or more of these wants underlie many of our distressing thoughts, feelings, and reactions. It can be helpful to delve a bit deeper to identify which of these basic wants may be operating for you in a given situation and then work on releasing and letting go of the thoughts and feelings related to that basic want.

To understand how to apply this method to the fear of public speaking or performing, let's consider an example: Let's say you just learned that you have to give an important presentation or performance in the near future. Your mind and body react strongly, and you experience a range of distressing thoughts, feelings, and sensations. You feel dread in the pit of your stomach, and a feeling of intense fear and foreboding comes over you. Your mind starts to race and you wonder if you can somehow get out of participating in this event. Your chest tightens and your heart starts to beat rapidly as you contemplate what is up ahead. You imagine how incredibly overwhelming all of this is going to be, and you start to feel trapped and helpless—and then frustrated and upset with yourself for having these reactions.

Let's say that at some point in this scenario you are able to see yourself heading into the abyss (the earlier you catch yourself the better, of course) and you take a step back. You pause and take a slow, deep breath and recall the method of releasing and letting go: Rather than condemning yourself for having these thoughts and feelings, you give yourself full permission to be exactly where you are in this moment, no matter how bad it feels. Then, after a few moments of full, unconditional acceptance of where you are, you gently and slowly ask yourself the following questions, giving yourself time to fully experience each question: *Could I let this go? Would I let this go? When?*

You accept whatever genuine response comes, knowing that you may not feel ready, willing, or able to release and let this go right away. You welcome your response and let it be okay in this moment. You might repeat the cycle of questions one or more times, if you feel this might help you loosen the grip of whatever is happening a bit more.

You might also consider the basic want that is underlying your thoughts, feelings, and reactions—is it the wish for approval, the wish for control, or the wish for safety and security? It may even be a combination of these wants, though one may be stronger than the others. You can then welcome that basic want and give it permission to be there, then ask yourself the three questions again to see if you are able to let go of the basic want that is driving your current distress.

One of the Sedona Method® questions that I have found helpful, especially when I find myself resisting letting go, is *Would I rather have freedom and peace of mind right now or would I rather hold on to my distress and continue to feel bad?* Inevitably, this question reminds me that it is my choice and that at any moment I can decide to free myself of my distress and welcome back my peace of mind by releasing and letting go.

I invite you to work with this method around your distressing thoughts, feelings, and reactions related to speaking or performing, as well as any other areas of life that create tension, stress, and pressure for you. I also encourage you to learn more about the Sedona Method® by visiting **www.sedona.com**.

Guiding Intention: I work on reclaiming my peace of mind by consciously choosing to release and let go of my inner distress.

Affirmative Thought: I am aware that at any moment I can choose to release and let go of my distress about a speaking (or performing) event.

Practice: With eyes closed or open, reflect on the distressing thoughts and feelings you have related to your public speaking or performing anxiety. Give yourself full permission to have these distressing thoughts and feelings without resisting the feeling of discomfort or judging yourself for having such a reaction. Sit with these unpleasant thoughts and feelings for a moment or two, and then gently invite yourself into the releasing and letting go process by slowly asking yourself the following questions: *Could I let this go? Would I let this go? When?*

You may want to continue to slowly and gently ask yourself these same questions, in the same order, as it may take a few rounds of the releasing process to loosen the grip. It may be helpful to use the exercise of putting something in your hand that represents your inner distress and tightly gripping your hand around this item, then asking yourself the same three questions as you gradually loosen your grip and ultimately release whatever you were holding so tightly.

You can also practice this method to help release and let go of any basic wants that may be underlying your distress by asking yourself: *Is this about the wish for approval, the wish for control, or the wish for safety and security?* You can then go back to the original three releasing questions to work toward letting go of one or more of these basic wants that are at the core of your distress.

Remember not to try to force your desired outcome, as that would be counterproductive to the more gentle process of releasing and letting go. Let whatever unfolds be okay, even if you discover you are not fully ready to release and let go of the distress yet. If a part of you is still holding on and not yet ready to let go, repeat the same process by giving yourself full permission to be where you are at in each moment (or come back to it at a later time). Gently ask yourself the questions again related to letting go of the need for things to be different or resolve faster than they are right now.

If you are feeling resistance to releasing and letting go of your distress, you may also want to reflect on the question: *Would I prefer my freedom and peace of mind right now or would I rather hold on to this upset and continue to feel bad?*

Be sure not to judge yourself negatively if you continue to hold on to your distress for the time being, realizing that most of us resist letting go and that it can take time and patience if the resistance is strongly held. Be gentle with yourself and persistent in working with the process.

CHAPTER EIGHTEEN

States of Mind That Limit or Expand

As we have already seen, our mind can work for us or against us. And when we are in a state of high anxiety, or any other negatively charged feeling state, the mind is clearly not working in our favor. Our strong negative emotions limit and distort our perception of reality. We tend to believe in, and become identified with, our thoughts and perceptions as though they represent truth, and we easily lose touch with a more objective and rational experience of reality.

When we are in this state of mind, our perspective on reality narrows and we may experience "tunnel vision" as we get lost in a haze of distressing thoughts and feelings. Our perceptions get further distorted as we identify with the stories our mind creates and experience these stories as real, rather than what they truly are—conjured up in our own mind. We easily lose touch with present moment reality as our mind associates to scary times in the past and projects frightening thoughts into the future (referred to as *what if* thinking). As we get lost in our dramas about all that is going wrong, has gone wrong, or may go wrong, feelings of helplessness arise and further compromise our ability to think clearly and adaptively.

It is said that the mind is delicate and we have to carefully tend to the mind and direct it, rather than give it free rein to go in any direction it wants. When our thoughts and feelings are agitated, we need to settle our mind before we are able to see things more clearly. An analogy aptly describes the experience of an agitated, clouded mind. Imagine a glass of water with sand and dirt particles floating in the water. If you keep stirring the water, it remains cloudy because of the sand and dirt. The water naturally clears when you stop stirring and allow the particles to settle to the bottom of the glass.

The mind behaves in a similar manner. When we keep stirring up our inner agitation by continuing to feed our mind negative thoughts and images, our mind becomes clouded and we cannot see ourselves or our situation clearly. We have to stop stirring things up and let the mind settle before we can regain clarity and objectivity.

It is not easy to settle the mind once the agitation starts. An agitated mind often feels like a whirling vortex that sucks you in and pulls you along by the force of its emotional strength. The agitation gains momentum from our conditioned, unconscious reactions, and once this force is in motion, we often feel at its mercy. At times it may even feel like we are in a trance, taken over by this emotional force inside of us and having no conscious awareness or control over the direction it is heading in. We are often overcome by a feeling of powerlessness, which greatly limits the mind's options and often leads us to respond in passive and avoidant ways that do not serve us.

Our best chance to break these strongly conditioned patterns of reactivity is when we become conscious of what is happening inside of us and can then slowly begin to redirect the mind. One way to start this process is to step back and adopt the curious observer or witness position. From this position, you watch what is going on inside of you as if you were a neutral third party, letting go of your identification with your internal experience and any judgments about what is happening within you.

Taking a step back and observing your thoughts and emotions in a dispassionate way frees the mind from the trap of believing in, and identifying with, its self-created dramas. This allows your mind to expand beyond its narrow, limited view and gain perspective on what is really going on. When you take the role of a curious, neutral observer of yourself, it helps you to not take yourself and your circumstances so seriously and not believe all that your mind conjures up when it is agitated and caught in a flurry of emotion.

As we pause and detach a bit from the inner workings of the mind its agitation naturally begins to settle and we gain clarity and perspective. Then we are in a much better position to redirect our mind toward a more positive and resourceful focus, which strengthens its capacity to better serve us. We can redirect our mind away from what is sometimes referred to as "small mind" and toward what has been called "Big Mind."

Small mind—the condition of having a constricted, limited view of self, others, and the world—happens especially when we are preoccupied with our ego concerns. It often creates the illusion of not being enough or having enough, and it fuels our feelings of insecurity and inadequacy. Big Mind—the condition of having a wide, open view of ourselves, others, and the world—is cultivated when we consciously shift our focus off of our self-concerns and more deeply and fully connect with ourselves, others, and the vast world around us. When we are able to step into the more expansive view of Big Mind, we tend to no longer feel so personally threatened and in need of protecting our ego concerns. As we relax our self-protective stance we are better able to see more clearly, think more clearly, and connect more deeply.

The cultivation of Big Mind is supported by a regular meditation practice, as well as the practice of mindfulness (present-moment awareness) in daily life. Assuming the position of a neutral observer of the mind also supports the development of Big Mind. These practices help you to become more aware of the inner workings of your mind, which frees the mind to access a deeper truth and broader perspective about what is going on within you and around you.

When our mind becomes agitated by upsetting thoughts and feelings, we need to become conscious of what is happening as quickly as we can, disengage from our self-created stories and dramas, and recognize that our agitated, "small mind" is distorting our thoughts and perceptions. We need to not be lured into believing in these thoughts and perceptions as representing the truth simply because they have such a strong emotional charge and feel true in the moment. We can work toward settling the anxious, agitated mind by not stirring things up even more. Instead, we can pause, take a deep breath, and disengage from our inner drama by adopting the role of the witness. This allows us to step back and neutrally observe what is playing out in our mind rather than being helplessly carried along by its dramas.

As our mind settles, we begin to gain calmness and clarity, and then we are able to see a deeper truth and a broader perspective. This process naturally moves us away from small mind and toward a Big Mind perspective, where we feel a deeper connection and gain a clearer, more expansive view of ourselves, others, and the world around us.

Guiding Intention: As I become more aware of the inner workings of the small mind I am less identified with its stories and dramas.

Affirmative Thought: I create a Big Mind perspective whenever I am facing a speaking (or performing) challenge.

Practice: Anytime your mind starts to get agitated or you feel increasingly anxious about a public speaking or performing challenge (or any other life circumstance), see this as a golden opportunity to practice shifting from a small mind to a Big Mind perspective.

First, notice how coming from a small mind perspective affects your experience of public speaking or performing. Instead of passively "going along for the ride" by believing in and identifying with the stories and dramas in your mind, see if you can pause, take a deep breath, and mentally and emotionally detach from the small mind perspective.

Now, imagine your mind moving beyond this limited view and opening up to the broader, more expansive perspective of Big Mind, and envision what is possible from this view of yourself, others, and your circumstances as you approach a speaking or performing event. Imagine approaching all future speaking or performing events from a Big Mind perspective and viewing your experiences through this more expanded state of mind.

CHAPTER NINETEEN

Inquiring into the Mind's Thoughts and Beliefs

OUR MIND HAS AN ARRAY OF STRONGLY HELD BELIEFS WHOSE ROOTS go far back into our early personal histories. As was mentioned in a previous chapter, the foundation of our belief system is strongly shaped by our early life experiences and is especially influenced by our interactions with significant others, and how we interpreted what we experienced.

From this foundation, our mind has gravitated toward certain patterns of thoughts and feeling states that continue to support and reinforce the beliefs we hold. We tend to automatically believe in what we think and feel as though it were true, simply because it has been such a central part of how we have come to see ourselves and our world. A problem arises, however, when we hold onto beliefs that are based upon faulty ways of thinking and allow these beliefs to go unchallenged even though they adversely affect our lives.

I have found The Work of Byron Katie very useful as a framework for inquiring into the unquestioned mind and examining the deeply held thoughts and beliefs we hold as true. Katie came upon this method of inquiry into the mind after suffering a long history of depression that significantly impaired her functioning for many years. After much suffering, she suddenly understood her core problem, which was that she believed in, and her life was driven by, some deeply held negative beliefs and patterns of thinking that were simply not true.

As Katie began to inquire into her mind and deeply question the basis of these distressing thoughts and beliefs, she was able to challenge the validity of the thoughts and beliefs that were causing her much stress and deep unhappiness. Once she deeply understood and accepted that these disturbing thoughts and beliefs were not really true, she was freed of the grip of these stressful thoughts and beliefs and the emotional toll they were taking on her life.

Katie's first book, *Loving What Is*, outlines the method she teaches. Four basic questions guide the inquiry into the way the mind thinks and believes something to be true, as follows:

1. *Is it true?*
2. *Can you absolutely know that it's true?*
3. *How do you react when you believe that thought?*
4. *Who would you be without the thought?*

Let me offer an example of applying this to one of the stressful beliefs I hear over and over again from people who have a fear of public speaking or performing—that people in the audience will think less of them and lose respect for them, and they will lose credibility, if they appear highly anxious when speaking or performing. If we were going to question the truth of this belief using the method of The Work, the inquiry would go as follows:

Is it true? You may say *No* to this question if you are able to step back and see this differently just by the conscious act of reflecting deeply and questioning the truth of this belief. If you still honestly believe that it is true (or may be true) and say *Yes* to this question, then you would proceed to the next question.

Can I absolutely know that it's true? Chances are pretty good that you will respond with *No* to this question, as there is no way to know with absolute certainty that everyone would respond this way unless you polled each person in the audience and every one of them said they would lose respect for you and see you as lacking in credibility. This seems highly improbable indeed. Some people might feel this way, but it seems very unlikely that everyone would.

How do I react when I believe that thought? Chances are you would respond by naming many stressful thoughts, feelings, and behaviors, such as, *I worry about what people are going to think of me if they see how anxious I really am.*

I value my reputation and don't want to lose credibility and respect, especially of people whose opinions I highly value. I feel even more anxious as I think about this happening. I feel frustrated with myself over having this fear. I feel like avoiding the situation and many times try to get out of it if I can. I feel helpless over this fear and hate the fact that I feel this way!

Who would I be without the thought? Chances are you would respond to this question by listing thoughts, feelings, and behaviors that feel much better and ease the pressure and stress you are feeling, such as, *I would feel much more relaxed and at ease. I would feel less anxious. I would feel I can just be myself and do the best that I can and not be worried about what others think of me. I would be more able to focus on my real purpose rather than worrying about how I am coming across and how others might be judging me. I would feel free at last!*

Katie also speaks of three alternative ways of thinking, called "turnarounds," which help to loosen any rigidity around stressful and disempowering thoughts and beliefs and view them from a fresh perspective. She classifies the turnarounds as follows: turn it around to yourself, turn it around to the other, and turn it around to the opposite. She invites you to experiment with the different turnarounds and to notice how they can feel just as true, or perhaps truer, than the original thoughts and beliefs.

An example of turning it around to yourself in this instance would be to substitute *I* for *the audience*: *I will think less of myself and lose respect for myself, and see myself as less credible, if I become highly anxious when speaking or performing.* This turnaround helps us see that we often project onto others what we are experiencing within ourselves and invites us to own our own feelings and thoughts, rather than believe we can know the feelings and thoughts of others. In fact, Katie has noted that what others are thinking and feeling is not even our business, unless they choose to share them with us. We have to mind our own business and pay closer attention to what we are thinking and feeling, instead of thinking about what is in the minds of others. Once we own our thoughts and feelings, we can inquire into the truth of the beliefs underlying them and begin to let go of beliefs that are not true and do not serve us.

An example of turning it around to the other in this instance might be: *I lose respect for others when I project my fearful thoughts and feelings onto them and don't recognize they have the capability of responding to me in a more mature and supportive way.*

Finally, an example of turning it around to the opposite might be: *Others shouldn't have to respect me and value me to bolster my self-esteem if they genuinely don't feel this way. It's up to me to build my self-respect and confidence from within myself and not be reliant on what I believe others may be thinking and feeling about me.*

I invite you to look further into Byron Katie's work and to use her method to deeply question the stressful thoughts and beliefs that you hold as true. When we inquire into the nature of these unquestioned thoughts and beliefs, the fog starts to lift and we can see more clearly what is really true and what is just illusion. You can learn more about Katie's work by visiting her web site at **www.thework.com.**

Guiding Intention: I choose to inquire deeply into the truth of my stressful thoughts and beliefs and not simply believe in them because they feel true.

Affirmative Thought: I am able to free myself of my stressful thoughts and beliefs about public speaking (or performing) and create new ones that are based on a deeper truth.

Practice: Find a quiet place away from distractions and interruptions. Spend a few minutes relaxing as you breathe slowly and deeply. Consider the most stressful thought and belief that you have around public speaking or performing and write this down, using words that most clearly capture how you hold this thought and belief in your mind. Now, write down your responses to the four questions, as follows:

1. *Is it true?*
2. *Can you absolutely know that it's true?*
3. *How do you react when you believe that thought?*
4. *Who would you be without the thought?*

Then come up with three turnarounds that feel just as true, or perhaps truer, than your original stressful thought or belief, as follows:

1. *Turn it around to yourself.*
2. *Turn it around to the other.*
3. *Turn it around to the opposite.*

Notice the effects of inquiring into one of your most stressful thoughts and beliefs and then questioning its very foundation by exposing a deeper and greater truth.

I encourage you to do this exercise with other stressful thoughts and beliefs you have about public speaking or performing. See if you can expose the distortions in these thoughts and beliefs and come up with more empowering ones that are just as true, or perhaps truer. While doing this inquiry may not immediately lead you to fully and completely let go of your stressful thoughts and beliefs, it will begin to loosen their hold on you.

CHAPTER TWENTY

The Law of
Attraction

MUCH ATTENTION HAS BEEN GIVEN LATELY TO WHAT PEOPLE are calling the Law of Attraction. In fact, there are books, audio recordings, and movies created to expound upon this powerful universal law (one of the most popular being *The Secret*, which is out in book, CD, and DVD formats). The basic idea behind this law is that "like attracts like," that we draw into our life experience whatever our mind focuses on in a persistent way, especially if there is a strong emotional charge to what we are focused on, either positive or negative. Referring to quantum physics, human beings are described as energetic beings carrying a certain vibration and they draw toward them life experiences that match that vibration, which is strongly influenced by the quality of their thoughts and feelings.

While the skeptical among us can debate the validity of this idea, many people seem to resonate with its basic premise. It is helpful to draw from our own life experience to make sense of its truth.

For example, when we are in a state of anxiety, pessimism, and self-doubt, and immersed in the thoughts and feelings connected to these states of mind, we feel a distinct difference in our life energy compared to when our thoughts and feelings support a joyful, optimistic, confident state of mind. When we are in a highly anxious or discouraged state, we often feel our life energy being sapped as our perspective narrows and we feel weighed down by worry and doubt. When we are focused on negative emotions like this, if something good comes our way we are unlikely to see it and allow it into our experience. By contrast, when we are in a joyful, uplifted, positive state of mind, we often feel our life energy surge as our perspective on life expands and amplifies the good, making it easier to allow and even invite more positive experiences into our lives.

The idea behind the Law of Attraction is to consciously direct our mind and emotions toward what we want to attract into our lives and shift our attention away from what we do not want (which is a similar idea to what we discussed in an earlier chapter). Because the unconscious mind tends to be very literal, we attract toward us whatever we are focused on, even if it is what we want to avoid. So if we focus on our worries and fears about what could go wrong, we are more likely to attract these things into our life experience by virtue of giving such emotionally charged attention to these possible negative outcomes. Even if we do not end up manifesting them in our external reality, we often feel as though we have had a very negative experience because our mind, body, and spirit have been so enveloped in this anxious, fearful state that it has felt very real to us.

Those of us who have experienced high levels of performance anxiety are strongly conditioned to think and react in negative ways when it comes to public speaking or performing. We easily fall into this way of thinking without even realizing it, as it has become such a familiar, automatic response. It takes much conscious awareness and determination to redirect the mind toward a positive view when we feel so anxious and afraid, as the pull toward the negative is often very strong.

The good news is that with persistent effort, the mind can be reconditioned. Brain research has discovered that the adult brain is more capable of learning new patterns of thought, feeling, and behavior than previously believed (so you can teach an old dog new tricks after all!). As we practice positive patterns of thought, feeling, and behavior we build and strengthen new neuropathways and create certain neurochemicals in our brain that make it easier to access these new pathways over time. At the same time, we are decreasing our tendencies to reinforce the old neuropathways and are less influenced by the neurochemicals associated with negative and fearful thoughts, feelings, and behaviors, so these pathways weaken and have less of a hold on us. In essence, we are imprinting new patterns in our mind.

There are a variety of ways to work on creating a more positive mindset and focus of attention to allow the Law of Attraction to work in your favor. The earlier chapters in this section of the book highlight a number of them, and we will review a few more in the chapters that follow. One of the first steps in making this shift is to increase your awareness of the nature and quality of your thinking—put it on your "radar screen" as something you monitor—as your habitual ways of thinking will take over if you are not paying conscious attention. You then need to remember, and apply, the principle behind the Law of Attraction, which is to direct your mind as much as possible to that which you want to attract into your life and spend as little time as possible giving attention to that which you do not want.

For instance, if you catch yourself being pulled into negative thoughts about a public speaking or performing event, deliberately shift your focus of attention to thoughts about how you want things to go and the positive feelings and behaviors you would like to experience. Even if you feel skeptical and do not believe or trust that good things can happen for you around speaking or performing, *act as if* you do and refocus your mind to seek out and encourage more uplifting and empowering thoughts, feelings, and behaviors.

An analogy regarding airplane navigation comes to mind. When a plane is traveling toward its desired destination, it actually gets off course many times en route. It finally arrives at its desired destination through an ongoing series of "self-corrections," where the pilot closely monitors the path it is traveling and makes adjustments any time the plane gets off course. Likewise, we have to monitor our mind closely and self-correct any time we are not going in the direction of our desired destination, which would be to have more positive and empowering experiences with speaking and performing (in the inner world of our mind as well as our external reality).

One thing I know for certain is that anxiety, negativity, and self-doubt are way off course and allowing our mind to travel down that path takes us further away from our desired destination. When we self-correct as soon as possible by aligning our focus, attention, and energy in the direction of our desired outcome, we are engaging the Law of Attraction in our favor. In doing so, we create an energy and vibration within us that attracts and allows more positive internal and external experiences with speaking and performing, as well as in any other area of our lives in which we apply this same principle.

Guiding Intention: I engage the Law of Attraction to work in my favor.

Affirmative Thought: I easily attract and allow positive feelings and experiences with speaking (or performing) as I direct my mind to focus on the positive outcomes I want to create.

Practice: Write down a list of your typical thoughts related to public speaking or performing (you will likely know these very well by now if you have done the prior exercises in this section!). Also write down the feelings and behaviors that arise from having these thoughts. You might title this page "Allowing the Law of Attraction to Work against Me!"

On a second sheet of paper (or in your journal), counter each negative thought, feeling, and behavior with an opposite one that is empowering and uplifting. You might title this page "Allowing the Law of Attraction to Work in My Favor!" If coming up with empowering thoughts, feelings, and behaviors is not easy, you may have to *act as if* you believe a positive experience is possible, which is perfectly fine if this helps to move you in the direction of a more empowered mindset.

Notice the differences between the two lists, and then put an X through the first list and rip it up, as you will not want to put any further attention on it. Stay focused on reading your second list, closing your eyes to imagine creating your desired thoughts, feelings, and behaviors from this list. Remember, it is fine to *act as if* you believe these positive outcomes are possible for you if you are not quite there yet with believing you can have what you want.

Imagine these positive outcomes as vividly as possible in whatever way works best for you. Try to create strong positive emotion as you imagine magnetically attracting toward you what you want. Ideally, repeat this exercise many times over the coming months, imagining your desired outcomes moving toward you easily and effortlessly as the power of the Law of Attraction works in your favor.

CHAPTER TWENTY-ONE

Setting SMART Goals

MANY OF US WANT THINGS TO CHANGE FOR THE BETTER WITH REGARD to our public speaking and performing challenges—and perhaps challenges in other areas of our lives as well. However, rather than clearly identifying what we want and laying out a specific plan of action to get it, we may handle our wish for change more like a hope or a prayer.

I recently heard Jack Canfield speak on the topic of goal setting. He mentioned a study of high achievers that showed that the act of deciding what you want and writing down your goals in a specific, measurable way—and reviewing and visualizing your goals with positive expectation each day—increases your chances of achieving what you want by as much as two hundred percent! He noted that most people do not do this, and so they miss out on using a strategy that could move them light years ahead.

In addition to defining your goals clearly and specifically, a further step is needed: the willingness to take sustained, positive action that moves you in the direction you want to go. This willingness to "pay the price" to achieve your desires in life is a hallmark of top performers who have a track record of success in achieving their goals. What stops many people from ultimately achieving what they want is resisting letting go of the comfort of old habits and not wanting to feel that uneasy and scary feeling as we step outside of our "comfort zone."

While changing our old ways often brings some level of anxiety and discomfort, we clearly pay a different sort of price by staying stuck in our old ways that no longer serve us, limiting our functioning and the realization of our potential. The good news about the change process is that the accompanying anxiety and discomfort are usually short-lived. Once we become familiar with the new way of being, we regain a measure of comfort once again, as well as a hefty dose of confidence and empowerment for having stepped up to the challenge rather than backing away from it.

While setting well-defined goals has not usually been my style, I have recently found this practice very useful in helping me get clear on my priorities and the best use of my time to achieve what is important to me. Defining goals in this way—deciding what is most important and the best way to get from where you are to where you want to be—is another example of living a more conscious life. Many people who are serious about achieving their goals use a system such as SMART goals, which is an acronym for:

Specific—*setting specific goals, which have a much greater chance of being accomplished than goals stated in vague, general terms*
Measurable—*using concrete criteria for measuring progress toward your goals*
Attainable—*deciding what steps you need to take that will make reaching the goals that are most important to you possible (and probable)*
Realistic—*choosing goals that you are willing and able to work toward achieving*
Timely—*creating a realistic time frame to achieve your goals.*

Some of us may be good at setting SMART goals in other areas of our lives but find ourselves floundering when it comes to public speaking and performing. We feel lost, frustrated, and helpless, as whatever we have tried did not seem to work. We may find ourselves giving up and simply avoiding the situation as much as possible, rather than problem-solving as to what other steps we could take to make progress. At times like these, when we feel at a standstill (or a dead end) with our own efforts, it helps to brainstorm with others who may be able to offer fresh ideas. While it is ultimately up to us to take the steps to achieve our goals, it can be very helpful to seek guidance along the way and be able to benefit from the support of others.

One success strategy used by many top performers is to have a system of support and accountability in place, as it is easy to let goals slide as we get caught up in the busyness of daily life. A system of support and accountability keeps our goals on the radar screen as a high priority and sharpens our resolve in taking the sustained actions needed to achieve our goals. There are various ways to build that support and accountability for yourself, including finding an "accountability buddy" with whom you can share mutual support, working with a coach, or working with a group of like-minded people in a mastermind group. Many of us pride ourselves on our independent spirit and are used to going it alone, though in doing so we miss out on the incredible support and camaraderie available to us.

Working on your goals involves both making inner changes in your attitude, beliefs, and thoughts and creating the external changes that relate to taking action on a behavioral level. One high-impact method of promoting inner change used by many top athletes and high performers is positive visualization and imagery. In *The Success Principles: How to Get from Where You Are to Where You Want to Be* (a book I highly recommend), Jack Canfield speaks of visualization as "the most underutilized success tool you possess," and he notes that practicing visualization "greatly accelerates the achievement of any success." Unfortunately, all too often we use visualization and mental imagery to our disadvantage as we picture in our minds all the things that could go wrong. This negative imagery ends up feeling very real to us and leads us to lose faith and confidence in ourselves as we come to believe these outcomes might really happen.

Instead of allowing our fear and self-doubt to lead the way, we need to consciously direct our mental imagery to allow us to see and feel things happening the way we would most like them to happen. This practice has a powerful effect in priming the mind to move us toward the fulfillment of our goals. The impact of positive visualization is further amplified by consciously creating strong positive emotion as we visualize achieving our goals. If you find it hard to believe in this positive imagery from where you stand right now, simply *act as if* you believe it were true with a genuine, good-faith effort and you will begin to see the power of this practice.

Finally, the change process happens most powerfully and effectively when you follow up the inner changes you are making with regular, sustained action in the outer world. In the case of public speaking or performing, this would mean making a plan to put yourself in speaking or performing situations of increasing challenge and applying the methods you are learning to reduce and better manage the feelings of fear and anxiety that arise. While you can make progress by working on the level of inner change or outer change alone, there is a powerful synergy that happens when you actively work on both levels simultaneously, and you gain a much greater benefit from this more integrated approach.

Guiding Intention: I clearly define my goals and use positive visualization and sustained action to achieve what is important to me.

Affirmative Thought: I am making progress by changing on both inner and outer levels as I approach speaking (or performing) challenges.

Practice: Try using the SMART system of goal setting to create clearly defined goals with manageable time frames related to your speaking or performing challenges. It is best to write down your goals in your journal, or on a pad of paper or index cards, rather than just think about them. You may have just one specific goal you would like to focus on right now, or you may have multiple goals you want to achieve in this area of your life.

For each goal you write down consider what inner changes you need to make as well as the outer actions you need to take to achieve your goal. Write these down as clearly and specifically as possible with a time line of when you will actively work on these areas. Create your goals and lay out an action plan in a way that feels achievable and motivating to you. Be sure not to overwhelm yourself by setting the bar too high, or fail to inspire a healthy level of challenge by setting the bar too low.

Consider what sources of support and accountability you can put in place to keep you focused and moving forward in a sustained way and take action on creating this for yourself.

Try using positive visualization and mental imagery to pave the way for positive results. It is most ideal to do this practice one to two times each day for a few minutes at a time (preferably soon after awakening in the morning and shortly before going to sleep at night). Don't worry if you are not good at visualizing. Simply close your eyes and create in your mind as vividly as you can the image and feelings of a positive experience of the goal you are visualizing. Imagine taking the required actions and manifesting your goal exactly as you would like it to happen. And remember to *act as if* you believe in what you are visualizing, even if it feels like a real stretch from where you are at now to where you want to be in the future. As you move closer to your goal this gap will begin to close and the results you are after will feel more believable and achievable.

CHAPTER TWENTY-TWO

Taking and Sustaining Action

GETTING INTO ACTION AROUND THE GOALS WE HAVE CREATED for ourselves can sometimes feel daunting. At times we may get ourselves to initiate action and the bigger challenge becomes sustaining positive action over time. We tend to be creatures of habit and often gravitate to what we find most comfortable and familiar. We often come up against a fair amount of resistance when faced with taking actions that bring us outside of our comfort zone and cause us to stretch ourselves in ways that we are not used to. At times we may find ourselves procrastinating, or completely avoiding taking action in the areas of our lives that are difficult and challenging for us, such as public speaking or performing.

It is tempting to avoid the things that make us feel uncomfortable, especially if they make us feel highly anxious and afraid. We get an immediate sense of relief when we back away from them, and that feeling of relief is strongly reinforcing as it leads us to feel comfortable, safe, and secure again. The problem with backing away from our difficulties and challenges, however, is that it strongly limits us and does not allow us to discover and express our fullest capability and our highest potential in life.

Feel the Fear and Do It Anyway, the title of a book by Susan Jeffers, PhD, captures a good principle to live by if you want to develop personally and professionally and not have fear limit your potential. We often hold the mistaken belief that people who seem comfortable with speaking or performing—or other activities that require taking risks and stepping outside of one's comfort zone—somehow find it easy to do, and that they do not feel anxious and afraid. The more I read and hear of the experiences of highly successful people who have achieved much public recognition, the more I believe that virtually everyone feels some degree of fear and anxiety when stretching themselves into unknown and unfamiliar territory. The people who take action despite their fear have learned to tolerate the feelings of anxiety and discomfort and to "feel the fear and do it anyway*." It seems that in the very act of doing the things we are afraid of we are able to tap into our inner resources and discover a strength we did not know we had.

Some of us have felt the fear and have done it anyway, yet we have not found this to be an empowering experience, which leads us to want to follow the path of avoidance even more. The difference between whether taking action is going to feel empowering or disempowering relates to how you perceive the challenge and what you choose to focus on, which ultimately shapes your feelings and perceptions.

People who find taking action empowering, despite the anxiety and discomfort they face in the process, tend to validate, affirm, and reinforce the good in the situation and not focus on all that is uncomfortable, scary, frustrating, or disappointing. By contrast, people who feel worse after taking a difficult and challenging action often focus on and reinforce all of the unpleasant, scary, and distressing feelings. In doing so, they tend to magnify and deepen the unpleasantness of the experience, leading them to want to avoid at all costs ever going through something like that again.

When people are experiencing a phobic level of fear and avoidance behavior, it is even more tempting to avoid taking action in the area of their feared situation so as not to risk having feelings of panic or loss of control. While this is very understandable, as no one wants to feel such intense and unpleasant feelings, the avoidance behavior itself becomes part of the problem as it ultimately reinforces and deepens the cycle of fear and self-doubt.

While it takes a lot of determination and courage to step forward and do the thing we are most afraid of, taking action in this way ultimately helps us to overcome the limitations that fear imposes in our lives. And the best way to get ourselves to take action in areas that are highly charged with fear is to break the actions down into small, manageable steps; use helpful strategies to better manage the fear and anxiety that arise; and create accountability, support, and positive reinforcement for ourselves.

One way to chunk down actions into smaller, manageable steps is to create a behavioral hierarchy. This is often done by ranking different actions on a scale from 1 to 10, where 1 represents the lowest level of fear and anxiety associated with a specific action and 10 represents the highest level. It is important to come up with specific action steps for each progressive level of challenge. A sample hierarchy of action steps in the area of fear of public speaking or performing might look something like the following (note that your own hierarchy may look quite different from this basic template as you tailor each step to your individual circumstances):

1. *Participate voluntarily in a casual, small group discussion (or performing situation) outside of my work situation*

2. *Participate voluntarily in a casual, small group meeting (or performing situation) at work*

3. *Briefly introduce myself (or perform) in a casual, small group situation where I am expected to speak (or perform), rather than it being voluntary*

4. *Introduce myself (or perform) in a more formal, small group situation where I feel the expectations are higher than in a more casual setting*

5. *Present (or perform) in a more formal small group meeting (or performance situation) in front of people I am comfortable with where I am well-prepared and feel confident with my competency with the material*

6. *Present (or perform) in a more formal small group meeting (or performance situation) in front of a small group of my peers with whom I feel less comfortable presenting (or performing)*

7. *Give a formal presentation (or performance) in front of a larger group of people outside of my work situation where I feel the expectations are not so high*

8. *Give a formal presentation (or performance) in front of a larger group of my peers where I feel there are higher expectations*

9. *Give a formal presentation (or performance) in front of those who hold higher status or power where I feel the expectations are even higher*

10. Give a formal presentation (or performance) in front of a large group of my peers and those who hold higher status or power where I feel the expectations are higher still

The behavioral hierarchy gives you a road map and allows you to get clear on the progressive actions you can take to move toward your larger, more challenging goals. You can also create subgoals and repeat a number of actions at each level as many times as you need to gain confidence before advancing to the next level of challenge. Of course, in the real world we don't always have the luxury of taking smaller steps before we are faced with more challenging situations. Despite this, it is still helpful to define your own personal hierarchy and do the best you can to proactively take progressive actions to build your confidence as you move toward the bigger challenges you face.

It is also helpful to consider the ways you can mentally prepare yourself to manage the fear and anxiety that arise when you are taking action. While progressively moving through the hierarchy helps to desensitize you to the feared situations and gives you more confidence, it is also important to use the tools you are learning to discover the strategies that best support you at each step of the way. In doing so, you are simultaneously working on strengthening your inner resources while also taking actions in the outer world—an ideal combination to desensitize yourself to the feared situations.

As I noted in the last chapter (and it bears repeating here), many of us try to go it alone when facing the big challenges in our lives, including the challenge of public speaking or performing. However, we are more likely to give up on our efforts when the going gets tough if we rely solely on ourselves for motivation and accountability. Many highly successful people have learned the art of getting support from others and having a system of accountability in place with one or more people so they are held to a high standard for follow through when facing their biggest challenges.

Some people create a relationship with a coach, colleague, or friend to ensure accountability. Other people may benefit from mutual accountability fostered in a group setting, as is the case with a mastermind group, where the members support one another in taking actions on the goals that are important to each of them.

Having a person or group to be accountable to can make a big difference in mobilizing you to take action when you are tempted to procrastinate or avoid. A person or group can also support, affirm, and encourage you to sustain your momentum and believe in yourself when you feel overwhelmed or discouraged in the face of your biggest challenges.

Many of us are very good at giving support to others yet find it hard to ask for and receive support for ourselves. I encourage you to create relationships that support you as you take action in this area of challenge, as well as a plan to acknowledge, celebrate, and reward yourself for your successes along the way—both big and small.

Guiding Intention: I take consistent, sustained actions that move me closer to my goal of speaking (or performing) with more confidence and ease.

Affirmative Thought: I step up to speak (or perform) despite any fear or discomfort I may feel.

Practice: Create a behavioral hierarchy for yourself in the area of public speaking or performing, listing specific actions you can take that are associated with varying levels of challenge. Use the 1-to-10 ranking system, with 1 marking an action that you can take that is associated with the least amount of fear and anxiety and 10 marking an action that creates your highest level of fear and anxiety. Fill in the rankings in between with increasingly challenging actions. Try to be as specific as possible and create realistic actions that are possible for you to take within the context of your work and life circumstances.

Create a plan to work slowly but steadily on your action list, starting with the least challenging action and progressively working up to the more challenging actions over time (though you may also work on this list in a different order based upon your circumstances). Create subgoals within each level if needed and repeat specific actions more than once, or many times, if you need to do that before feeling ready to move to the next level. Be sure to consciously practice and apply the strategies you have been learning to help you better manage each level of challenge as best as you can, rather than simply muscling your way through each action step.

Consider who can give you support and provide accountability for you so you are more motivated to take sustained, consistent action when the temptation arises to procrastinate or avoid. Be sure to put this support and accountability in place right from the beginning so you have the best chance of working through your hierarchy from start to finish. Once you have completed it, you may want to create another hierarchy for yourself when you feel ready to start again, hopefully from a much higher starting place the second time around. And, finally, be sure to acknowledge and celebrate your successes along the way!

SECTION THREE
SPIRIT

CHAPTER TWENTY-THREE

Relaxing the Need for Control

GO WITH THE FLOW AND LET WHATEVER HAPPENS BE OKAY IS A helpful saying to think about whenever we feel a loss of control. Following the wisdom of these words helps us to let go of the struggle we may be having with our inner experience (if we are not feeling as we would like to feel) or our external circumstances (if they are not going the way we would like them to go). This saying reminds us to relax and let things unfold rather than try to control inner conditions and outer circumstances to suit our wishes and expectations.

Many of us who experience performance anxiety are strong-minded achievers who have difficulty letting go and surrendering control when things are not happening in a way that we would like them to. We often feel increasingly tense and frustrated as we struggle to regain a feeling of control over our inner experience and outer circumstances. While this is true for many people, with or without performance anxiety, people who are high achievers often have a stronger need for control—and more difficulty surrendering control—than people who are less driven by high expectations for themselves and their lives.

While the need for control can operate as a strength, propelling us to accomplish more and rise to higher levels of achievement, it can also work against us by creating much frustration and anxiety when things are not proceeding according to our hopes, plans, and expectations. At those times, we may strongly resist what is happening and "argue with reality," wanting things to go our way. It is clear that when we argue with reality, we never win.

To stop fighting against *what is* and simply allow things to be the way they are, even when they are uncomfortable or anxiety-provoking, is in fact very freeing. It is immediately relaxing to the mind and body when we let go of our resistance to what is happening and our wish for things to be different, especially when we do not have immediate and direct control over our circumstances. The Serenity Prayer, attributed to Reinhold Niebuhr, captures the essence of this spiritual teaching:

> *God grant me the serenity*
> *to accept the things I cannot change;*
> *courage to change the things I can;*
> *and wisdom to know the difference.*

The practice of letting whatever happens be okay is not meant to encourage passivity and helplessness or just taking whatever comes our way. Rather, it is meant to relax the need to control and change unpleasant conditions as an automatic reaction to our feelings of discomfort. It helps us pause, step back from being reactive, and simply accept *what is* in the present moment.

Once we neutralize our reactivity to whatever we are resisting and let it be okay just as it is, it no longer has a hold on us. As we let go of the need for control, we become less emotionally charged and more able to see things clearly and calmly. It then becomes easier to turn our attention to identifying the things that are within our control—including our perceptions, attitude, thought process, and behavior—and finding the courage to take action on changing them.

Learning to accept *what is* can be very challenging, as the natural tendency is to resist what we do not like and do not want. It takes much patience and practice to unlearn reactive tendencies. Yet developing the more conscious and measured response of pausing, stepping back, and accepting things as they are is well worth it, as it is the most immediate and direct way to re-establish a feeling of calm and control within ourselves. Paradoxically, the conscious choice to surrender control is often the very thing that gives us a feeling of having more control rather than less.

We often become caught in a control struggle, feeling that either we have to control this problem and its symptoms, or the problem and symptoms will control us. The struggle to control our inner experience leaves us emotionally exhausted, and we usually end up feeling even more anxious, discouraged, and defeated.

Rather than wage a war against the fear, the better thing to do is to raise the white flag and surrender. Let it be okay that you have this problem and these symptoms. Let it be okay that you feel anxious before or during a speaking or performing event. Let it be okay that people might detect your anxiety—and even that they may judge you badly because of it. I understand this is not your preference, and I can assure you it is not mine either. We all prefer to feel calm, confident, and at ease, and for people to see us at our best. But we cannot flip a switch and have this happen as we want it to, so the next best thing is to let it be okay where you are right now and to stop fighting against yourself and your current reality.

I want to emphasize that this does not imply that you become complacent and not attempt to work on this issue. Rather, letting go is a starting point from which to create a more relaxed, supportive mindset and to work with our fear and anxiety in a kinder, gentler way. Once we feel this inner support and acceptance, and can surrender our fight for control, we are more able to relax and go with the flow. When we are not struggling to gain control, or desperately trying to hold on to it, we naturally find our way to a more calm and relaxed presence. Being relaxed and in the flow is much more likely to bring out the very best we are capable of at any given moment, ultimately leading us to feel more in control of ourselves and our circumstances.

Guiding Intention: I practice accepting the things I cannot control and taking steps to change the things I can control.

Affirmative Thought: I go with the flow and let whatever happens be okay whenever I approach a speaking (or performing) event.

Practice: Become more aware of your reactions to your inner state and outer circumstances that don't match your wishes or expectations, especially around public speaking or performing experiences. Note any tendencies to "argue with reality" and tense up as you resist and react to what is happening in those moments. See if you can engage a more conscious mind and pause, step back, and reflect on the saying: *Go with the flow and let whatever happens be okay.* See if you can practice the wisdom of those words, reducing your reactivity about whatever is happening and simply allowing things to be exactly as they are.

Note any shifts in your feelings and state of mind when you consciously choose to surrender your need for control. Also feel what it is like to simply go with the flow rather than fight against what is happening. Continue to practice this approach in your daily experiences with difficult people and circumstances, as well as during your public speaking or performing challenges. Feel the serenity that comes as you accept situations that are not within your immediate and direct control. Then take the next step and further develop your wisdom and courage by defining what is within your power to influence or control and taking steps to effect those changes.

CHAPTER TWENTY-FOUR

Leading
with Heart

WE LIVE IN A SOCIETY THAT STRONGLY VALUES THE MIND, where intellect and high achievement are greatly revered and a competitive, goal-focused person is often admired as someone who is on the fast track to success. Many high achievers are more strongly connected to their heads than to their hearts, especially when they are striving toward success in achieving their ambitions. When we are driven by our ambitions, and our need to excel, we are more strongly identified with our ego than we are with our heart. We often become overly concerned with ourselves, and with how we are being perceived by others, and less attentive to the feelings, needs, and concerns of others. When we are driven by our need to succeed and be held in high esteem (and the need to not fail and risk losing respect from self and others), we tend to lose touch with a deeper, more genuine heartfelt connection with ourselves and with our fellow human beings.

When our ego concerns take the lead—related to our strong need to protect our image and reputation and to be respected and thought of highly by others—we view others from a very self-centered frame of reference. When we place so much significance on what others think of us, and greatly fear the possibility of their negative judgment, others become extensions of us and we make the situation all about ourselves. In doing so, our perceptions of people get distorted and we lose touch with the basic humanness of others and the feelings, needs, and concerns that are important to them. In fact, when experiencing high levels of performance anxiety, we may become so self-conscious and self-preoccupied that we almost forget that anyone else but us exists, other than thinking about them as our judges or critics.

When we are in this self-centered, ego-driven state of mind, we often feel very separate, alienated, and alone. We are not able to connect with our own heart energy or feel the comfort of basic, human connection with others, which makes it increasingly difficult to find any solace during those times.

Connecting with heart energy is a very grounding and healing experience. I often refer to this heartfelt connection as "coming back home" to yourself, where you become less focused on superficial ego concerns and, instead, connect more deeply with yourself and others from a heart-centered place. Connecting with heart energy allows for a more genuine and meaningful connection. Relating to ourselves and others from this place provides much peace and comfort and has the capacity to calm and center us at our deepest core.

One pathway to connecting to your heart is finding a softer place inside of you, leading you to relate to yourself in a kinder, gentler way. Instead of coming down hard on yourself with frustration and disappointment when you are highly anxious, or if you have had a difficult experience where you felt you let yourself down, it is more helpful to soften toward yourself and assume a compassionate, forgiving stance. This is akin to what a loving, nurturing parent would do with a child who is scared or feels he or she failed at something. Rather than be harsh and unforgiving toward the child, or focus on the child's perceived shortcomings, the parent would assume a soft, gentle, heartfelt presence to help soothe and comfort the frightened, distraught child.

This heart-centered approach is deeply soothing and comforting to all of us and is what we need to give to ourselves, especially at our most vulnerable times. When we are faced with high anxiety and fear, or feelings of disappointment and failure, rather than hardening against ourselves with tension, frustration, or anger, we need to soften and be gentle and kind toward ourselves. We need to soften around our uncomfortable feelings of anxiety and fear, as well as soften toward ourselves for not having met up to our hopes and expectations for ourselves. It is vital that we feel our own inner support at times of fear and vulnerability and do not turn against ourselves. This heart-centered approach is like a healing balm for the soul. It will begin to naturally ease feelings of fear and anxiety, or discouragement and defeat, as we relax our hard edge and treat ourselves with compassion and kindness when we are facing our most trying times.

Leading with heart also refers to how we relate to others. It means we begin to connect more deeply with the basic humanness of all people. We feel a more heartfelt connection with others as we experience the commonality of our human experience on a deeper, more fundamental level.

Leading with heart means we look more deeply at people and see their basic humanness behind their title, their status, or whatever else intimidates us or distances us from them. It means we relate to people as individuals, rather than project all sorts of feelings and judgments onto them because of their external roles or life situations. Leading with heart also means we willingly and generously share our knowledge, skills, and talents to help support and empower others. It allows us to care about others more deeply as we are moved to contribute what we can for the good of others, letting it become about them rather than about us.

As we open our heart, speaking or performing becomes a very different experience. Rather than feeling separate and alone as a speaker or performer, we feel a bond and kinship with the individuals in the audience as we connect with them on such a fundamental, human level. When we are coming from this heartfelt place, the fear tends to naturally dissolve on its own.

Guiding Intention: I open my heart and treat myself with compassion and kindness whenever I am anxious and afraid or feel discouraged and defeated.

Affirmative Thought: I lead with my heart whenever I am speaking (or performing).

Practice: Take a few moments to sit or lie down in a quiet, undisturbed place. Close your eyes and put one hand on your heart, using a soft, gentle touch, and the other hand on your belly. Breathe deeply, slowly, and fully into your heart center and allow the breath to expand a feeling of softness and openness around your heart. Then, imagine directing your breath downward and guiding this heart energy deep into the area of the belly, feeling a safe, open, and grounded feeling radiating from your core.

Connect with this heart energy any time you feel anxious and afraid or discouraged and defeated. Soften around these uncomfortable feelings and around any areas in your body or mind where you tend to harden, tense, or tighten against these feelings. You might imagine the touch of a soft, warm blanket or something else that represents softness, warmth, soothing, and comfort. Allow the softness to surround these difficult feelings and provide a safe harbor for these feelings.

Finally, imagine leading with heart when you are in a speaking or performing situation. Imagine looking at individual people in your audience and feeling a deep human connection and a feeling of caring and compassion toward each person you look at. Think about the burdens many of these people are carrying in their lives as they struggle with any number of life problems and challenges. Consider the feelings of anxiety, fear, and vulnerability that we all share based on our experience of being human.

Recognize your kinship with the people in your audience and open your heart to them, realizing that they, like you, are doing the best they can with whatever challenges life has handed them. Feel your heart opening and softening as you feel a deep bond with your fellow human beings. Feel the genuine caring toward others as you willingly and generously share your knowledge, skills, and talents in your wish to help them in some way. Feel your ego concerns fade and become more distant as your heart takes the lead and you begin to care more about serving others than protecting yourself.

CHAPTER TWENTY-FIVE

Focus on Appreciation and Gratitude

WHEN WE ARE IN A STATE OF WORRY, ANXIETY, AND FEAR, we are focused on lack and limitation. We feel we are lacking in some way, and we fear that we will lose something that is important to us, such as our credibility, reputation, acceptance, approval, or respect. When we are in this mindset, we have a very limited view of ourselves and our lives and feel as though we are not able to measure up to our own or others' expectations. We focus on what we feel is wrong with us or what might go wrong when we face difficult and challenging situations.

This focus on lack and limitation distorts our view of ourselves and our lives and leads us to miss the bigger picture of who we really are and all that we have going in our favor. It also leads us to distort our view of others, projecting a harsh, critical, judgmental reaction coming from others as we imagine them seeing us as lacking in some way. When we project such a negative view onto others, and perceive them as our judges and critics, we miss the opportunity to experience any understanding, acceptance, support, and kindness they might express toward us if they were to see us as anxious or vulnerable.

When our mind is held captive by these distortions, it is as though we are caught in a trance of fear and darkness. We quickly lose touch with a more favorable and optimistic view of ourselves, our lives, and our experience of others. It is important to awaken from this trance and regain perspective so we can perceive a much truer and more accurate view of ourselves, our lives, and our beliefs about others. We need to consciously remember what is true about ourselves and others in a more whole and complete sense, rather than perceive ourselves and others in such a narrow, limited, and fragmented way.

One very helpful way to refocus the mind during these times is to direct your mind away from your perceived flaws and hardships and toward your strengths and blessings. Actively paying attention to things you appreciate and feel grateful for about yourself and your life, and your experience of others, allows you to access your spiritual nature and raises you to a higher level of consciousness very quickly. It brings you almost immediately into a more positive, expansive state of mind. It also opens your heart to feelings of comfort and ease, which allows you to see and appreciate how much is truly good and right with yourself and others. As you connect with the abundance that is present and available to you, your spirit is uplifted and your fear and anxiety naturally begin to dissolve.

Another way to create feelings of appreciation for your life circumstances is to call upon the principle of relativity. It can be helpful to reflect upon your life situation and the challenges you face relative to the life circumstances and challenges of so many others who are less fortunate or who face higher levels of stress, pressure, and burden. It has been said that the problems we face in our society are "first world problems" and that we are very fortunate to have the challenges that we face rather than the survival challenges that so many people in less developed countries must cope with.

Even if you compare your life situation to those whose life circumstances seem more fortunate, you can always come up with a way to appreciate your life challenges relative to the bigger challenges and higher level demands many people face each day. For example, if you are feeling stressed about an upcoming presentation or performance and you are starting to blow it out of proportion, think of people who have far more pressures and demands in their lives and far more at stake, such as presidents of nations or other high-level officials. Or consider people who have far greater personal challenges to contend with, such as those who have a major illness or who have just lost a loved one.

In reflecting upon the many people who have problems and challenges to manage that are of far greater magnitude, we can immediately regain perspective on our own challenges and recognize how much smaller and more manageable they are relative to those of many others. It is good to remind ourselves of how very fortunate we truly are, even in the face of our most difficult challenges.

When we are in a state of fear and negativity, and focused on lack and limitation, we often have the feeling of a burdened, heavy heart and a dark view of life. By contrast, when we shift our focus to one of appreciation and gratitude—and appreciate all that is good and right about ourselves, our life circumstances, and our experience of others—our heart begins to open up and our mind and body feel more spacious, lighter, and brighter. This higher-vibration state of appreciation connects us with a more spiritually grounded feeling and a sense of wholeness and completeness, even with the imperfections in ourselves, others, and our lives. When we are connected to this deeper, more expanded state of being, fear and anxiety tend to dissipate easily and naturally on their own, without effort or struggle.

Like most things, cultivating a state of appreciation and gratitude takes practice, as many of us have fallen into the habit of taking our lives for granted or focusing on feelings of limitation or lack, especially when we are facing our most difficult challenges. I invite you to reflect upon and appreciate your many blessings each and every day and discover the magic that happens when you create more conscious awareness of just how fortunate you really are, even in your darkest moments.

Guiding Intention: I focus on all that I am grateful for about myself, my life, and others, and take nothing for granted.

Affirmative Thought: I remember to appreciate my strengths and the many blessings I have in my life as I face my speaking (or performing) challenges.

Practice: Find a time each day to focus on appreciation and gratitude. Take a few moments to reflect upon all that you appreciate about yourself—your personal qualities, your accomplishments and achievements, and the choices you have made along the way that have worked well for you. Consider all of the blessings you have in your life as well—your health, your home, the conveniences you have available to you, and the many other aspects of your life that bring you comfort and joy.

Reflect upon what you appreciate about others—both people that are close to you and who you know well and people who you don't know well (or at all) but who extend gestures of kindness or friendliness when you encounter them. Train your mind to notice these things and to appreciate them rather than take them for granted.

Any time your mind gravitates to thinking about flaws and limitations concerning yourself and your life, or negative projections onto others, remind yourself to look for the good and appreciate the "glass half full" rather than the "glass half empty." We typically find what we are looking for, so if we look for faults and things to be worried about, we generally find them. By contrast, if we look for things to appreciate, we find an abundance of things to feel grateful for. Consider the small things as well as the bigger things of life, not taking even the smallest things for granted.

You may want to keep a log of your reflections on appreciation and gratitude to further reinforce this practice. And, on days you feel especially fearful, anxious, or gloomy about an upcoming presentation or performance, or for any other reason, you may want to review and add even more to your list so you flood your mind with positive, uplifting thoughts and feelings to raise your spirit and your "vibration" to a higher level. You may also want to bring your list with you to your presentation or performance and keep it close by as a reminder to pay attention to the good rather than focus on any feeling of lack or limitation.

CHAPTER TWENTY-SIX

The Blessings
of Adversity

DURING DIFFICULT AND CHALLENGING TIMES, IT IS HELPFUL to recall the wisdom of looking for the hidden blessings in the midst of our struggle. Two sayings that capture the essence of this message are: *The most difficult people and circumstances in our lives are our greatest teachers* and *Every adversity carries with it the seeds of equal or greater benefit* (the last saying is attributed to Napoleon Hill; I am not certain who coined the first saying). When encountering a person or a situation that is very unpleasant or difficult to bear, recalling the wisdom of these words helps to direct our mind to look for the lessons and opportunities embedded in these challenging circumstances.

Rather than letting these situations fuel feelings of fear, anger, frustration, or discouragement, it helps to view them as a spiritual practice—an invitation to learn and practice some important life lessons and skills. Instead of feeding off the negative thoughts and feelings we may have about our difficult circumstances, it helps to bring a conscious mind to these unwelcome situations and to learn whatever the obstacles and difficulties have to teach us.

While most of us prefer feelings of comfort, security, and ease, and dislike anything that disrupts our peace of mind and our feeling of having control over our lives, it is the most difficult and challenging people and circumstances we encounter that move us out of our comfort zone (in fact, sometimes *way* out of our comfort zone) and create the potential for our greatest personal growth and development.

If we were to embrace the belief that our most difficult circumstances are our greatest teachers, and that every adversity has equal or greater benefits, we would approach our experience of performance anxiety very differently. Rather than wishing away our problem and strongly resisting (and resenting) our experience, we would instead look for the important lessons that can be learned as we try to navigate our way through this challenge. Instead of turning against ourselves in disappointment, frustration, and anger when we are feeling anxious and afraid, and wishing we could climb out of our own skin, we would use this challenge to cultivate a more kind, compassionate, and supportive response toward ourselves when we are facing our most frightening and difficult moments. We would see the hidden blessing within this challenge as an opportunity to build a much stronger and deeper level of caring and support for ourselves and to learn to unconditionally accept and stand by ourselves, no matter what.

When looking for the benefits in this adversity, we would come to see the blessing of learning to accept our humanness and not needing to run away or hide from the parts of ourselves that we dislike or are uncomfortable to experience. (These are often referred to collectively as *the shadow self*, as we try to hide our undesirable qualities both from ourselves and from others.) The more we can be with those parts of ourselves that we wish were not there, and come to accept and embrace the less desirable parts of our being, the more we are expressing unconditional love and acceptance toward ourselves (rather than just accepting ourselves conditionally—when we feel strong and in control). When we see our challenge as our greatest teacher, we discover many important lessons we can learn in cultivating a deeper relationship with ourselves as we truly are (rather than always chasing the image of our ideal self) and many valuable coping skills that can help us in all facets of life.

As we create a more accepting and supportive relationship with ourselves within the context of our own life struggles, we tend to also cultivate a more understanding and compassionate attitude toward others who struggle in life. As we become less judgmental toward ourselves when feeling vulnerable, we tend to become less judgmental toward others as well. We are often able to develop a deeper empathy and compassion toward people facing life challenges, connecting more with the shared human experience of facing difficult feelings and circumstances. The qualities of understanding, compassion, and empathy toward ourselves and others reflect important aspects of personal growth and maturity and are often developed more in the context of facing adversity than in times when we are feeling strong and in control.

In addition to the lessons of deeper understanding, acceptance, and compassion, there are other lessons to be learned and skills to be developed in facing this challenge. As we reflect more deeply upon our experience of this fear, we have a chance to learn more about ourselves and our personality that may be limiting us. We may discover such things as perfectionist tendencies and having expectations of ourselves that can be too high at times; being hard on ourselves when we don't meet our own expectations (and also possibly being judgmental toward others when they don't meet our expectations of them); being overly serious and overly invested in our reputation and public image; placing too much importance on what others think of us and on gaining their acceptance and approval; being guarded and fearful of exposing our perceived flaws; finding it difficult to trust that people will accept and respect us if they see any flaws or vulnerabilities in us; and fearing taking risks that might lead to any public display of failure on our part. Self-awareness is the first step toward change, and as we become more aware of the different facets of our personality and our approach to life, we have a better chance of changing things that may not be serving us.

We may also discover more about our feelings and reactions to those who possess power and authority. Many people who have performance anxiety feel intimated and diminished around people who hold more power or status than they do in their work life or in other areas of life. We often regress into a child-like state of mind around these people and elevate people who have power and authority into a parentlike, or even Godlike, position. We tend to hold these people in high esteem by virtue of their position and status and create an idealized image of them, failing to see their humanness or experience our shared human connection.

As we become more aware of our projections onto authority figures, and our anxious attempts to please authority, we can learn more about ourselves and continue the journey of personal growth and development. Just as a maturing person begins to view his or her parents more objectively and accept the full range of their strengths and limitations, we can learn to have a more mature, adult view of those who hold positions of power and authority. Instead of idealizing these people, we can look more deeply and see the truth of their humanness, connecting with them on a basic human level rather than elevating them above us and feeling intimidated by them or guarded in their presence.

It is important to change how we respond to our most difficult problems and challenges. Rather than resist adversity and see it as an intruder in our lives, robbing us of our peace of mind and feelings of control, we can begin to see adversity as an invitation to achieving higher levels of personal growth and maturity. Instead of succumbing to feelings of frustration, helplessness, and discouragement, we can use our difficulties as opportunities to cultivate and practice higher-level coping skills and to develop more mature attitudes and behaviors that will serve us well going forward.

From adversity we can learn to calm and ground ourselves when we feel agitated and off balance. We can discover how to be resilient and solution-focused, putting our full attention on finding ways to get right back on track whenever we have veered off course. We can learn to unconditionally accept and support ourselves in our most difficult moments and let go of striving for perfection and complete control over ourselves and our lives. We can come to know more about ourselves and how we approach life, which creates an opportunity to change whatever does not support us in living our best life. We can become more patient, kind, and supportive toward ourselves when we are in the midst of our distress and not functioning at our usual capacity. And, among the many other lessons, we can develop heartfelt compassion and empathy as we more deeply connect with others, recognizing and appreciating our shared human experience of facing challenge and adversity at times in our lives.

Guiding Intention: I look for the benefits in adversity and the lessons I can learn from the most difficult people and circumstances in my life.

Affirmative Thought: I see the adversity and difficulties of my public speaking (performing) fear as an invitation and opportunity to grow and mature.

Practice: Reflect upon the idea that the adversity of having performance anxiety holds many benefits for you and that the difficult circumstances you encounter with this fear bring many opportunities for your personal growth and development. Take some quiet time and journal on the hidden blessings this adversity holds for you in the form of lessons to be learned about yourself and others, the deepening of your relationship with yourself and others, and the many skills that you can develop and nurture as you navigate your way through this challenge.

Anytime your fear and anxiety get triggered, see if you can remember to regard these uncomfortable feelings as an invitation to learn and grow, rather than react in your usual way by fighting or resisting these feelings. Consider the lessons you can learn each time the feelings arise, and use these times as opportunities to develop more self-awareness and to practice better coping skills. You may want to keep a running log of the many benefits you discover as you face this challenge with less reactivity and a more conscious mind.

Develop the mindset of "mining for gold"—looking for hidden blessings whenever fear and anxiety arise rather than feeling victimized or oppressed by these feelings. You may want to extend this mindset to adversities and encounters with difficult people or circumstances in other areas of your life as well and take a more conscious approach to how you face all difficult challenges that life brings your way.

CHAPTER TWENTY-SEVEN

Generosity and Contribution

ONE OF THE PRINCIPLES I WROTE ABOUT IN MY FIRST BOOK IS often referenced by my coaching and workshop clients as having the biggest impact in reducing their speaking or performing anxiety. That principle is: *It's not about me!*

Those of us who experience high levels of performance anxiety have often come to view a speaking or performing event as all about ourselves. We see it as a proving ground for ourselves, and we fear failing in some way and suffering public humiliation. We are afraid of personal loss, especially the loss of our good reputation, our credibility, and the respect of others. We are often much less concerned about our mastery of the material we are presenting or performing, which most of us feel pretty confident about, and far more concerned about having our feelings of high anxiety and deep vulnerability exposed to others.

Most of us have prided ourselves on being pretty "together" people, with many successes and accomplishments to our credit. We have tended to form an identity around our successes and accomplishments and the control we have demonstrated in our lives. We have great difficulty accepting this feeling of deep vulnerability and loss of control, which is so contrary to how we normally experience ourselves and how we are perceived by others, and we are often terrified at the thought of exposing this hidden part of ourselves to others.

Whenever we become fearful of losing something important to us, our survival instincts kick in and we tend to get self-protective and watchful over possible threats to our safety and well-being. When feeling threatened like this, we tend to become preoccupied with ourselves. This self-absorbed, guarded stance leads us to put up mental barriers, which creates distance between ourselves and others and leads us to feel separate, isolated, and alone.

The more we desperately try to protect ourselves from the perceived threat we are running from, the further alienated we become from the real people and the real situation we are facing. In our moments of high anxiety and panic, we end up feeling very frightened and alone in our small, self-created world of threat and danger. We project these unsafe feelings onto others and the situation we are facing, believing they pose the real threat to us, though in actuality it is our distorted perceptions, beliefs, and thoughts that have created the threat we are experiencing.

At times we may lose complete touch with the true reality that is in front of us as we regress into a childlike state and come to believe in the monsters in our mind. We are drawn further into this regressed state as we experience feelings of helplessness and powerlessness and lose touch with the more accurate perception of reality that we normally experience when inhabiting our adult state of mind.

When we are in this childlike, regressed state, we become egocentric and believe the world revolves around us. We are not able to see other people as separate and distinct from their experience of us, just as a child is not able to see a parent figure as having his or her own separate life apart from the child's. When we are in this regressed state, we see things as a frightened child would see them, and we feel the helplessness and powerlessness that goes along with the deep anxiety a child experiences when feeling completely lost and alone.

One of the best ways to pull out of this regressed state, and to anchor ourselves in our higher-level adult functioning, is to shift our focus away from ourselves and onto others. We need to wake up from this childlike trance and make efforts to reconnect with our adult perspective, reminding ourselves about the true reality of the situation. In the case of public speaking or performing, we need to focus on our true purpose in speaking or performing and to remind ourselves this is not about us; rather, it is about whatever information, inspiration, or enjoyment we can provide for others.

Even if a speaking or performing situation has a direct evaluation component and feels very personal (as might be the case with interviews, auditions, or exams), it is still important to shift our focus off ourselves and our personal concerns about succeeding rather than failing, as this only serves to heighten feelings of pressure and tension, which often lead us to not be at our best. In this case, it is more helpful to shift to a positive focus, such as connecting with others and the material we are sharing in a way that feels authentic rather than striving to prove ourselves. Focusing on the wish to genuinely, and generously, share whatever we have to offer—rather than getting caught up with the fear of being tested or evaluated and worrying about not measuring up—allows us to relax and get into a better flow, leading us to be more effective in whatever situation we find ourselves in.

While some speaking and performing situations have a direct evaluation component, many of the ones we face are not about this at all (though we often make them into this type of thing in our mind). The true purpose of many, if not most, of the speaking or performing situations we find ourselves in is to contribute to others in some way—to share information and knowledge, to motivate and inspire, or to entertain and create a time for enjoyment and pleasure.

Focusing on our true, higher purpose rather than our self-concerns is very reassuring, as we understand that our personal identity and self-worth are not on the line each time we get up to speak or perform. We are not under a microscope being scrutinized by others, and we are not so transparent that people can see right through us and know what we are feeling deep within ourselves.

The more we make speaking and performing experiences about us, the more anxious we get as we try to prove ourselves and measure up to what we believe is expected of us. Then we become even more afraid that people will detect our high anxiety and discover we may not be as "together" as they may have thought. The more we take the focus off ourselves and, instead, shift our focus onto generously giving of ourselves and making a contribution for the benefit of others, the more grounded and connected we feel and the less anxious we become.

Further, as we focus on benefiting others and cultivate a genuine desire to give of ourselves to help other people, we engage our highest selves as we tap into the heart energy that is associated with generosity and contribution. Some of the most evolved people in our society regularly operate from a place of generosity and contribution and have very little concern about their own ego needs. These are people who don't feel threatened by the opinions or judgments of others and are able to see beyond the lower-level ego concerns that so many of us get caught up in. These people come from a place of good will and genuinely want to share whatever they have to assist humankind. They are generally people who have much humility and little ego-related pride, despite their notable abilities and accomplishments. They are less concerned with loss of reputation, respect, or credibility and more concerned with contributing fully and generously with their unique abilities and talents for the benefit of the greater good.

While most of us are living far below this ideal in the way we experience speaking or performing, we can aspire to connect more with our spiritual nature and set a conscious intention to focus as much as possible on being a generous, loving, caring, and giving human being whenever we have occasion to speak or perform (and at other times as well). Creating this more spiritually grounded place within ourselves requires that we cultivate a willing spirit. Rather than feeling forced to speak or perform against our will, we can willingly choose to speak or perform as an act of generosity and contribution. We can *act as if* we were coming from this more spiritually evolved place and model ourselves after those who are devoted to generously contributing to humankind, even when our ego concerns lead us to not feel so generous of spirit.

When we set a clear, focused intention to come to our speaking and performing experiences from a place of higher purpose, and with a willing spirit, we create a more expansive and uplifted feeling that makes it easier to discover and follow this higher path. And each time we veer off this path and head down the lower road toward self-preoccupation with ego concerns, we need only become aware that we have gone astray and redirect our attention and focus to finding our way back to the higher road as quickly as we can.

Guiding Intention: I am a willing spirit and generously share my knowledge, talents, and skills for the greater good of others.

Affirmative Thought: I focus on my true and higher purpose of contribution and generosity whenever I speak (or perform).

Practice: Sit quietly in a comfortable, undisturbed place and take a few slow, deep breaths. Imagine a speaking or performing situation that you may be facing up ahead, or one that you have already experienced in the past. Create in your mind, and feel in your body, the experience of coming to this event with the baggage of your ego concerns—your self-preoccupation around your fear of losing your credibility, good reputation, or respect (or whatever other fears you have about how you will be perceived and judged by others). Connect with the feeling of being an unwilling spirit—feeling resistant, forced against your will, controlled by an outside source, and trapped in a situation you don't want to be in.

Feel how much this self-absorption and resistance distances and alienates you from a connection with others and how isolated and alone you feel when caught up in making this event about you. Observe how this self-preoccupation increases anxiety, self-consciousness, and self-doubt. Notice how coming from the position of an unwilling spirit deepens your fear and leads you to withhold and limit what you are willing to share of yourself as you try to protect and armor yourself from others.

Now, take a deep breath and shake off your resistance, fear, and self-preoccupation. Revisit the same situation of speaking or performing, but this time come from a higher-level intention to share openly and generously from a place of wishing to contribute and to benefit others. Consciously and deliberately create the feeling of a willing spirit—feeling open, cooperative, generous, and willing to step forward, graciously accepting whatever is being asked of you.

Take the perspective of the people in your audience, recognizing that all they really want is to learn from the person speaking or enjoy some pleasure in a performance they are attending. Feel a heartfelt connection with the people in your audience and create a sense of caring about them and a wish to give to them in a genuine and generous way. Imagine warmly giving of yourself to help others who simply want to learn and enjoy themselves and who are not there to pose a threat to you.

Act as if this were your experience even if it is hard to access these feelings right now. Feel the difference as you come from this more spiritually grounded and evolved place, where you are generous and expansive, as you freely and willingly offer whatever you have to give for the benefit of others. Notice how the focus on connecting, giving, and caring creates a more relaxed flow state and brings you closer to others and more in alignment with your highest and best self.

CHAPTER TWENTY-EIGHT

Moving Beyond Comparing and Competing

MANY OF US HAVE A COMPETITIVE NATURE AND SET THE BAR pretty high for our goals and achievements. Some of us are highly competitive relative to others and feel driven to excel and be the best. Others of us are less driven by competitive strivings relative to others but still may hold very high personal standards and define our success by how closely we measure up to our vision of how we would like to be and how we think we should be.

When we get into the mindset of comparing and competing with ourselves or with others, we feel as though we are being tested and have to continually prove ourselves. We end up putting a great deal of pressure on ourselves to succeed, and we often become fearful of failing. We may experience this competitive striving in many aspects of our lives, including our professional lives, our academic pursuits, and sometimes even our personal interests and hobbies, or we may experience this striving only in certain areas of our lives, such as speaking or performing in public.

Whenever we get into a competitive mindset and focus on comparison with others or with our own ideal standards, we assume a judgmental frame of mind. Even if we are not harshly judgmental toward others, or toward ourselves, our focus is on weighing and measuring ourselves against others or against an ideal personal standard.

While this mindset can sometimes motivate people to excel, and may have a place in promoting high-level achievements, it often fosters a win-lose mentality and creates much self-imposed stress and pressure. This mindset can also put us into a "me against them" mentality and lead us to feel much separateness and divisiveness with others. A competitive mindset is characteristic of how the ego functions, as the ego is very concerned with self-importance and self-protection and is strongly attached to winning and greatly fears losing.

One of the things the ego is most fearful of is losing the respect of others, as well as our own self-respect, when we are losing at something rather than winning. The ego is often very prideful and defines personal worth and value through achievements and through acceptance and approval from others. The ego thrives on feeling highly regarded and respected—and even admired— and often leads us to equate loss of respect with loss of dignity and self-worth. The ego is very attentive to hierarchies, often leading us to seek out higher status and power and to fear the loss of any status or power. The ego is often intimidated by those who have greater status and power, which leads us to be especially fearful of being judged or evaluated poorly by those in positions of power or authority.

When we operate from a mindset of comparison, competition, and judgment, we become even more fearful when we are visible in the public eye. We become afraid of being exposed as *less than* in some way, with the threat of loss of dignity and respect if we do not meet up to the expectations of others or to the expectations we hold for ourselves.

We often become fearful that people will discover we are not as strong and capable as they thought we were, particularly if they see evidence of our anxiety, and that this will confirm our feeling that there is something wrong with us because we are not more in control of ourselves. The ego is very prone to shame, embarrassment, and humiliation whenever we experience feelings of limitation, weakness, and vulnerability. This leads us to desperately want to cover up and hide our flaws and human vulnerabilities and to feel terrified and humiliated if they were to ever be seen or discovered.

To rise above these ego concerns, we first have to become aware of them and consciously work to not fuel them any further in our thoughts and reactions. The more we move away from a competitive, judgmental stance regarding ourselves and others and, instead, focus our attention on collaboration, contribution, and being part of a team effort, the more we distance ourselves from our self-concern and self-interest. The more we step away from continually trying to prove ourselves—always trying to win (or not lose) the race and pass (or not fail) the test—the less stressed and pressured we become.

When we begin to relax and let our guard down a bit, we are able to see things more clearly and see beyond ourselves. We are better able to remember that the world is not revolving around us and that people are not spending inordinate amounts of time thinking about us, no matter how we do. We recognize that each challenge we face is not a test of our personal worth and dignity and that our self-esteem does not need to ride on our successes and achievements or on how others may perceive us or judge us.

The more we step back from an ego-driven mindset and put our focus on connecting with others, the clearer our vision becomes of ourselves and others. We are better able to allow ourselves to be human and to humanize others at the same time. We are able to feel a more genuine and deep interest in others, rather than being interested in others for our personal gain, or only when it suits us. We become more capable of relating to others on a deeper level and truly experience that we are all in this together, realizing that we are all more alike than different in our human experience.

We are also able to erase the arbitrary and divisive lines around status and power that separate people and put them into categories. We are able to level the playing field and not be intimidated by those who hold positions of status and power, nor think of them as "authority figures." We can give these people the appropriate respect associated with their positions without projecting all sorts of extra power and authority onto them. We are also not prone to devalue or diminish those who might have less status or power by virtue of their positions. We grant them the same respect and consideration as we do all others. We feel neither *less than* those who have higher-level positions nor *more than* those who hold positions of lesser status and power.

Stepping back from this judgmental, competitive mindset does not mean we will be less productive or less successful. In fact, most people are more productive and successful in the long run—not to mention happier and healthier—when they feel less pressure to prove themselves and less driven by the need to succeed or the fear of failure.

When we take the focus off our ego-driven wish to win and rise above others, or the fear we may lose and sink below others, we are more relaxed and can interact with others in a more genuine and collaborative way. When we are relaxed and focused on connection and mutual support rather than self-protection or self-interest, we are more able to be ourselves and be at our best. We are also more open and approachable and able to bring out the best in others.

We become more attractive to people when we are not so self-absorbed and when we show genuine caring and interest in others. People tend to be drawn to those who present themselves in an authentic way and who are seen as sincere and approachable. In fact, the quality of authenticity has been noted as a characteristic of many highly successful speakers and performers. The side benefit of being authentic as a speaker or performer it that it eases fear and anxiety when we are being more ourselves and relating to the audience in a way that feels most natural to us.

We create better relationships with people when we come from this co-operative, collaborative stance than when we come from a place of competition and judgment, where we are most concerned about self-protection and personal gain. Paradoxically, when we let go of trying so hard to win (or not to lose), and connect more with supporting a team effort, we are more apt to succeed, and the journey becomes much more relaxing, enjoyable, and empowering for all.

Guiding Intention: I focus on collaborating and connecting with others rather than on comparing, competing, or judging myself or others.

Affirmative Thought: I present myself in an authentic way and show genuine caring and interest in others whenever I am speaking (or performing).

Practice: Sit quietly in a comfortable, undisturbed place and take a few slow, deep breaths. Imagine approaching a speaking or performing challenge with the mindset of competition, comparison, and judgment relative to others or to your own ideal standards. Feel the stress and pressure of trying to prove yourself and seeing this as a test of your self-worth and dignity. Feel what it is like to compare yourself to others or to your own ideal standards and to be fearful of failing or not measuring up. Feel the fear you have about losing credibility and respect from others, and possibly your own self-regard and self-respect. Feel the added pressure and stress of feeling intimidated by those you perceive have more status and power than you and being especially worried about whatever judgments they may have of you.

Now, shake these feelings off and, instead, imagine coming to your speaking or performing challenge with a very different mindset. This new approach you are taking is based in being authentic and genuine as you focus on connection and collaboration. You have stepped back from your own self-interest or self-protection and, rather than being preoccupied with succeeding (or not failing), you care more about the needs and interests of others. You connect deeply with the people in your audience and care about everyone getting value out of the experience. You no longer view people as above you or below you. Instead, you connect more deeply with the humanness of others, without placing them on a hierarchy of status or importance. This is no longer a test or a proving ground for you but rather a place to contribute and share with others so that everyone feels respected and empowered by what you have to offer.

Notice how much better it feels to approach speaking or performing experiences from a place of being authentic and connecting with others in a genuine, caring way rather than comparing, competing, and judging. Use future speaking or performing challenges as opportunities to practice this new approach.

CHAPTER TWENTY-NINE

Becoming the Observer
of Yourself

EACH OF US LIVES IN A SUBJECTIVE WORLD, WHERE OUR PERCEPTIONS create our reality. We tend to believe our experience of ourselves and our world as though it reflects the absolute truth about how things really are. We often create stories in our minds about ourselves, others, and what is happening around us, based on our assumptions, beliefs, expectations, and interpretations.

We seldom realize that these are stories—and that we are the creators of these stories—because what we think, feel, and believe to be true feels so real to us that we rarely question our experience of reality, even when we have evidence to the contrary. To see ourselves more clearly and objectively (rather than live in our mind-made stories), we need to get some distance from our thoughts, feelings, and beliefs and disengage from our subjective mind.

Sometimes we tell ourselves stories that feel good to us, and we feel happy and at peace with what we are thinking and believing. At other times, however, our stories lead us to feel much worry, anxiety, and self-doubt (as well as other negative feelings) and make it hard to trust in ourselves, others, and our life circumstances. In those cases, we may develop a self-protective shield around us. Often we are not even aware that we are walking around tense and guarded, not fully able to relax and flow with life. We find it especially hard to let down our guard when we are having difficulty trusting in our safety and security and feel the need to tightly control ourselves and what is happening around us.

When we experience high levels of fear and anxiety, or other undesirable emotions, we feel uncomfortable and want to get rid of these unpleasant feelings as quickly as possible. We often get frustrated and disappointed in ourselves for feeling these negative emotions, and we may judge ourselves as weak when we are not able to control what we are feeling. These self-judgments may be further compounded if we allow negative emotions to dictate our choices so that we avoid challenging situations or otherwise limit our full participation in life.

Many of us judge ourselves pretty harshly when we are not living up to our expectations of how we think we should be feeling and acting. We often have expectations about how our lives should be, and we may feel deep frustration and disappointment when our experience of ourselves is not matching our personal standard or vision (this is especially true for high achievers). At those times we may become self-rejecting and turn away from ourselves, particularly the undesirable parts of ourselves that we would like to disown (known as our *shadow self*).

Rather than trying to keep the less desirable parts of ourselves hidden, and feeling ashamed and embarrassed by them, it is much more healing and transformative if we can come to know and accept these shadow parts of ourselves and turn toward rather than away from ourselves at times when these parts of ourselves surface. At these times, it is most helpful if we can become curious, neutral observers of ourselves, stepping back from our judgments and reactions to what we are experiencing, and refraining from creating stories about what is happening.

Rather than make ourselves feel bad or wrong for feeling or being a certain way, it is far better to view ourselves and our experience from a position of openness, neutrality, and acceptance. Instead of relating to ourselves as a harsh critic might, we can approach ourselves with genuine curiosity as we try to discover how our mind works and uncover the stories we are telling ourselves about whatever is going on that is causing us distress.

Deeper levels of self-awareness, understanding, and compassion are possible when we let go of reactivity and judgment. We often cannot comfortably see things about ourselves or know our truest and deepest feelings, thoughts, and beliefs if we have a harsh internal critic ready to pounce on us and disapprove of who we are, especially when we are feeling most vulnerable.

In those moments when we are experiencing uncomfortable feelings or going through difficult experiences, it is often very helpful to assume this neutral observer position (sometimes also referred to as *witness consciousness*). It almost feels as though we are stepping outside of our own skin when we shed our immediate, subjective view of reality and become the curious observer of ourselves. We watch ourselves in a torrent of emotion, curious and interested in how our mind works, and even a bit humored by how we (and other human beings) are capable of creating such drama, especially when nothing external is really warranting our strong emotional reactions.

As we gain some healthy distance and emotional detachment from the inner workings of our mind, it is as though we are watching someone else caught in this self-created drama. As we learn to step back from ourselves and view ourselves more dispassionately, we become less reactive to our thoughts and feelings and less apt to buy into the stories we create. We are able to see ourselves more clearly and accurately and not take ourselves, or our inner dramas, so seriously.

Stepping back from ourselves and our stories with an open, neutral, curious stance frees us to know ourselves better and to deepen our understanding of how our mind works. It frees us from believing in all of our thoughts, feelings, and beliefs, as we realize that just because we think, feel, or believe something to be true does not mean it is grounded in truth and reality. It also allows us to be more self-accepting and forgiving toward ourselves as we lighten the hand of harsh self-judgment when we are being less than our ideal selves.

Part of nurturing unconditional acceptance and support of ourselves is being willing to honor all parts of ourselves—both the parts that feel good and are desirable to us and the parts that do not feel good and are not desirable to us. When we can simply become the witness of our experience and see ourselves as we are without judgment, we no longer label these less desirable attributes of ourselves as bad, wrong, or unacceptable. We then become willing to allow ourselves to be who we are without feelings of embarrassment, shame, or inadequacy.

When we let go of our stories and our judgments about how we should be, we are able to be more patient, kind, and forgiving toward ourselves for our shortcomings. This frees us to know, accept, and love ourselves as we are, embracing all parts of ourselves—both our strengths and our limitations.

Learning to be the neutral observer also applies to stepping back from the stories we create and the judgments we have about others and life situations. We can let go of our beliefs and assumptions about how others should be and how life should go and, instead, practice genuine curiosity and nonjudgment when people and situations are not in line with our wishes and expectations.

When we come from the position of a neutral observer, we are much more apt to see people and situations more clearly and objectively and respond to what is happening more calmly and adaptively. When we come from a place of judgment about how people and situations should be, we are much more likely to distort reality as we project our own expectations and stories onto others and life situations rather than seeing what is truly there. We also tend to be more reactive and stressed, which negatively affects how we handle ourselves in these circumstances.

Standing in the position of neutral observer, we are accessing a more spiritually evolved place within ourselves. We are willing to see, experience, and accept things as they are in this moment, rather than live in our highly subjective inner world with all of its expectations, judgments, and stories about how things should be. We are more able to flow with life and meet it on its own terms, rather than trying to control life and have it conform to our terms. Paradoxically, we end up feeling more relaxed and in control when we stop trying to control inner and outer forces, and our distressing thoughts and feelings often ease naturally and spontaneously.

Taking the position of an observer does not mean that we become passive participants in life and never try to influence what is happening within us or around us. It simply means we start from a place of accepting *what is* and are willing to experience and accept life as it presents itself—within ourselves and outside of ourselves. As we get some healthy distance from the inner workings of our mind, and become more self-aware and less reactive, we make more conscious and wise choices about how to respond most adaptively to whatever is happening within us and around us.

Guiding Intention: I practice being a curious, neutral observer and accept *what is* in the present moment, even the less desirable parts of myself and my life experiences.

Affirmative Thought: I emotionally detach from my feelings and reactions to public speaking (or performing) as I step into the role of an observer.

Practice: Take some time to reflect upon the distressing thoughts, feelings, and beliefs you have around your challenge with public speaking or performing. Allow yourself to feel the intensity and distress of the reactive mind.

Consider what stories you tell about yourself, others, and the situation when you are in this fearful state and how you tend to believe in these stories as though they are true. Notice how uncomfortable it is to be with the less desirable parts of yourself, known as *the shadow self*, and how you want to reject those parts and hide them from yourself and others.

Now see if you can emotionally detach from the reactive mind by getting some healthy distance as you think about the challenges you have with public speaking or performing. Imagine taking a big step back and moving away from the reactive, judgmental part of your mind.

As you gain more distance from the reactive mind, imagine taking the position of a curious neutral observer as you think about these challenges. Rather than getting caught in the drama of distressing thoughts, feelings, and stories, see if you can suspend these reactions and judgments for the moment and simply observe your experience with curiosity.

You might even want to imagine stepping out of your own skin for a moment and watching yourself as though you were a neutral third party, curiously observing someone else engaged in a personal struggle with this issue. Simply notice what this person (you) has been up against as he or she has been experiencing, and reacting to, this life challenge.

When you are facing an actual speaking or performing challenge, and any feelings of fear, anxiety, worry, or self-doubt arise, see if you can distance yourself and emotionally detach from what is happening so you don't get pulled in further by the momentum of what you are feeling. Once again, practice stepping back and taking the neutral observer's position, accepting *what is* in the moment. Rather than reacting to and judging any undesirable feelings or parts of yourself, imagine you can simply watch yourself having this experience from the position of a third-party observer who is not emotionally invested in what is happening.

Notice what it feels like to disengage and detach in a healthy way rather than getting caught in the undertow of an intense emotional experience. Notice how the conscious use of detaching emotionally by assuming the observer position can take the power and juice out of your intense feelings and free you from the feeling of being controlled by your emotional reactions.

CHAPTER THIRTY

Connecting with the Higher Self

AT TIMES WE OPERATE FROM THE MORE LIMITED PART OF ourselves, sometimes referred to as the Lower Self. This is the part of us dominated by our ego, which is always looking out for us and trying to protect us from possible threats to our safety, security, and well-being. The ego reacts quickly to feelings of vulnerability and is especially vigilant whenever we are experiencing states of heightened fear and anxiety.

In the face of true danger, we want our ego to be strong and alert, doing whatever it takes to protect us and keep us safe. When we are fearful of public speaking or performing, it is not our physical survival that is at stake. Instead, we experience the threat of a social and psychological loss—the loss of social acceptance and approval alongside the loss of self-esteem and self-respect. Remarkably, the possibility of a social and psychological loss seems to frighten us as much as, or possibly even more than, a physical threat.

When we feel threatened in this way, and our survival mode kicks in, the ego's self-protective mechanism is on red alert. We become highly self-focused and much attention is centered on keeping us safe and secure. Being in this state strongly pulls us into the experience of the Lower Self and leaves us feeling inadequate and insecure.

While the ego can limit us when we become self-protective and self-absorbed, a strong ego can also help us to accomplish much and strive for greater things. While the healthier part of the ego can motivate us to develop our personal strengths and inspire our highest achievements, the more protective part of the ego can lead us toward a superficial and limited view of ourselves and others. Being in this more limited state keeps us from knowing and experiencing a deeper, richer, and more solid connection to ourselves, to others, and to the world around us.

When we are perceiving things from the Lower Self, we feel separate and alone, and often quite vulnerable because of this sense of isolation. We may feel we have to make our own way all by ourselves and have to get ahead, and stay ahead, so we don't fall behind. This is a "dog eat dog" mentality, where everyone tries to get their fair share so they will not miss out or be left out in the cold.

This mentality is especially dominant in a highly competitive environment, and culture, which reinforces individuals' striving to get ahead and be the best. Operating from this mindset, we are so focused on looking out for ourselves that we often relate to others as a means to an end rather than deeply valuing and appreciating people in their own right. When coming from the limited view of the Lower Self, we often do not truly see others for who they really are as we filter them through the lens of our own self-concern and self-interest.

By contrast, when we come from a perspective referred to as the Higher Self, we experience ourselves, others, and the world around us in a very different way. We feel more grounded in, and connected to, our true essence. Our identity and sense of self are not based in our public image and reputation or concern about how others may perceive or judge us. We have a stronger sense of self that goes beyond these more superficial concerns. We care more deeply about being authentic and genuine rather than impressing others or proving ourselves.

Likewise, we value others more deeply in their own right and tend not to be judgmental or superficial in how we think about or relate to them. We go beyond the surface view and look more deeply at the real person apart from his or her role, title, or position. We are not focused on where someone stands in the hierarchy of status and power. We understand how insignificant all of this is in the bigger picture. Instead, we relate to all people equally with deep respect and empathy based on a genuine human connection.

Being grounded in the perspective of the Higher Self challenges our tendency to constrict our view to our own small world where we are the center of our universe. It reminds us of what is true, genuine, and meaningful in the larger context of our lives and the world around us. It helps us to connect with and honor our true self and to likewise connect with and honor the truth and basic humanness in others. It leads us away from our petty worries and concerns and gives us perspective as we are reminded of the bigger picture. It allows us to see how we fit into the grander scheme of things and leads us to be more interested in offering what we have to contribute for the greater good of all.

The Higher Self perspective helps us to gain a more accurate and realistic sense of ourselves, neither inflating our self-importance nor deflating our sense of self. It helps us to define and respect a healthy sense of self based on deeper and more enduring values rather than on superficial strivings or measures of success. It helps us to have empathy and compassion for others rather than judging or criticizing them. Coming from the Higher Self allows us to mature and build stronger character.

When we are feeling much fear and anxiety in relation to our public speaking or performing, we are strongly based in our Lower Self. In order to actively engage the Higher Self, we have to step outside the paradigm in which the ego operates when it feels threatened. Working on developing our spiritual nature helps to strengthen our connection to the Higher Self.

As we consciously engage the Higher Self, we become less concerned about our own self-interest and more concerned about how we can be of service to others. We experience the paradox that as we let go of the focus on protecting ourselves, we feel more safe and secure and less in need of protection. As we let go of our strong need to be in control, and appear in control, we end up feeling more in control. By letting go of our self-preoccupation and concern about how others may view us, we feel more deeply connected to others and less concerned about being judged. And as we connect more with the Higher Self, we are better able to let go of the narrow, limited perceptions and reactions that reside in the Lower Self, and we are finally set free of our fear.

Guiding Intention: I connect strongly with my Higher Self as I relate to myself and others in a deeper and more spiritually evolved way.

Affirmative Thought: I approach speaking (or performing) experiences from the perspective of my Higher Self.

Practice: Sit quietly in a comfortable, undisturbed place and take a few slow, deep breaths. First, imagine approaching a speaking or performing challenge from the perspective of the Lower Self. Notice the concerns the ego has about all of the possible losses you may suffer to your social standing and your sense of self. Notice the ego's need to protect and guard you from possible loss of social acceptance and approval or self-esteem and self-respect. Notice the feeling of needing to prove yourself and the fear of judgment that you experience when coming from the Lower Self. Notice the narrow, limited view you have in this self-protective mode and your inability to connect to the deeper, truer essence of yourself and others.

Take a deep releasing breath and shake off the feelings of threat and guardedness associated with the Lower Self. Now, imagine reaching for the higher realm of perception and connection associated with the Higher Self. Imagine connecting with your deeper, truer self and relaxing as you allow yourself to be who you truly are.

Imagine also experiencing others as they truly are, rather than projecting things onto others out of fear and insecurity. See yourself being able to connect with others more deeply and fully as a result of seeing them more clearly and accurately, separate from any self-concern.

Imagine letting go of your fear of being perceived and judged by others and, instead, relating to others in a genuine, heartfelt way. Imagine everyone benefiting from your active and full participation and feeling even more deeply fulfilled as you express your true potential naturally and generously.

See if you can consciously redirect your perceptions and reactions away from the realm of the Lower Self and take the higher road as you reach for the mindset and perspective of the Higher Self. Practice this any time you are facing a speaking or performing challenge, as well as at other times of stress and pressure when you would strongly benefit from this higher, more spiritually evolved, perspective.

CHAPTER THIRTY-ONE

Letting Go of Attachment to Outcomes

IT IS HARD TO BE NEUTRAL ABOUT THINGS THAT ARE IMPORTANT to us. We often have strong desires, preferences, and expectations about how we want things to go and how we want them to ultimately turn out. We often have equally strong assumptions about how our lives will be if things go our way or if they don't. We invest a lot of ourselves in our goals and expectations for our lives, and we can become very attached to the outcomes that we hope will come from our efforts.

If we perceive an outcome to be a success, we feel elated, and at times even ecstatic. This feeling may give us a bit of a high, however brief and fleeting it may be, and we feel a boost to our confidence and self-esteem as we experience the sweet glow of success. On the other hand, if we perceive an outcome to be a failure, we often feel discouraged, deflated, and demoralized, and our confidence and self-esteem take a blow.

We often personalize these experiences of perceived success and failure and end up feeling like they are statements about us. This is the danger of overinvesting and overidentifying with the outcomes of our goals and efforts—we end up getting overly attached to things turning out a certain way so we can feel good about ourselves and our lives.

As we try to pursue efforts that will lead to success, and avoid experiences that may bring feelings of failure, we can feel much pressure and stress. We often try very hard—sometimes too hard—to make things turn out according to our hopes and expectations. We may find ourselves feeling quite worried and anxious as we try to control the way things turn out, especially things that are very important to us.

We often have the illusion that we have full control over the final outcomes, even though there are many factors that we do not, and cannot, fully control. We usually know this, at least intellectually, yet we often still attempt to control things that are beyond our control, which triggers much worry and anxiety.

Much of the drive behind our overattachment to desired outcomes comes back to the ego and its need to feel strong and in control. The ego often feels wounded and deflated if we have an experience that we perceive as a failure or if things do not turn out in our favor. The ego is also prone to feeling helpless and powerless when we come up against feelings of not being in control, especially around things that are very important to us and things that are strongly connected to our identity and self-esteem.

When we feel a loss of control, we may begin to experience feelings of weakness and failure, and then become concerned about how others will judge us if we are not seen as successful and in control. The ego is afraid of anything that may lead us to feel (or look) weak and vulnerable, deflate our image, or tarnish our reputation. In fact, it will drive us even harder in the pursuit of success to avoid these unpleasant feelings and experiences. The more important anything becomes to us, the more anxious we become about the possibility of losing what we so strongly desire.

Perhaps the best response when we notice we are overly attached to outcomes is to become a bit more neutral about them. This does not mean that we become passive and do not try to put our best foot forward. It simply means that we make the outcomes of our goals and efforts less important to our fundamental well-being. We learn to not invest ourselves and our identity so strongly in the external outcomes we experience in life, whether positive or negative. We learn to not care quite as much, and not try quite as hard, to make things turn out just right so we can feel successful and avoid feelings of failure. We discover how to not take ourselves or our ambitions quite so seriously or to take things quite so personally. We relax and take the pressure off. We still care, we still try to do our very best, and we still prefer to have things turn out a certain way, but we come to realize that our external life experiences do not define who we really are at our core, and we learn to not base our identity and self-esteem on the positive or negative outcomes of our experiences.

Many of us know, either intuitively or through personal experience, that when we are more relaxed we are generally at our best. We can flow with life better and handle any pressures or challenges that come our way with more composure and ease. By contrast, when we are uptight and trying to control ourselves and outside circumstances, we usually experience much stress and tension, and this detracts from our being at our best. Needing things to go a certain way in order to feel good (and to avoid feeling bad) does not serve us well, though we often continue to fall into the same trap over and over.

We are much better served by putting forth our best effort to influence that which is within our control and then let go of the outcome and allow whatever happens to be okay. If things turn out as we prefer, we can experience this as a blessing and feel grateful for our good fortune. If things turn out in a way we do not prefer, then we can use this as a lesson in accepting *what is* and learning how to go with the flow of life. We can learn from our experience, not personalize what is happening, and not create a story in our head that leads us to feel even worse about ourselves and our lives.

Many times we try to control a situation due to fear of the unknown and difficulty dealing with uncertainty. Rather than experience the discomfort associated with not knowing how things will turn out—and the possibility that they may not go as we would like—we create hopes, wishes, and expectations and then try very hard to make things happen as we want them to. Once again, this puts us in the mode of trying too hard to control things, which is a recipe for worry, anxiety, and fear—especially fear of loss of control.

One saying I especially like that reminds us to let go of trying to control outcomes is: *Take care of the present moment and the future will take care of itself.* The less attached we are to the outcomes of our goals and efforts, and the more we surrender our strong need for control, the better able we are to deal with the unknown and the uncertain. We can flow with life in a more relaxed way and trust that we will be okay, no matter how things turn out. We find a healthy balance between putting forth our best effort and knowing when to let go and not care so much. Letting go of trying to control outcomes is a lesson in trust and is something most of us need to develop in the area of public speaking or performing, and possibly in other areas of life as well.

Guiding Intention: I let go of my attachment to outcomes and trust that I will be okay, no matter how things turn out.

Affirmative Thought: I take care of the present moment and let the future take care of itself whenever I face a speaking (or performing) event.

Practice: Take some quiet, undisturbed time to reflect upon any attachment to outcomes you may experience in public speaking or performing and the effect this has on you. Observe any need you may have to feel, and appear, strong and in control for the sake of your identity and self-esteem, as well as your reputation. Notice how you may attempt to control outcomes to avoid the discomfort of facing uncertainty or the unknown. Notice how you may personalize feelings of success or failure and experience them as though they are statements about your self-worth.

Observe any feelings of pressure and stress that arise as you experience yourself caring too much about the outcomes of your public speaking or performing experiences. Notice how it feels when you invest too much of yourself in concern about how you will be perceived and get overly attached to things turning out a certain way. Notice how it feels when you put your identity and self-esteem on the line and identify too strongly with feelings of wanting success (and wanting to avoid failure) in order to keep your self-image and self-esteem intact.

Now, take a deep releasing breath and shake off these feelings. Imagine letting go of any strong attachment you may have to the outcomes of your public speaking or performing experiences. Imagine becoming a bit more neutral and not investing so much of yourself, or caring quite so much or quite so deeply about how things go.

Instead, imagine having a preference for how things turn out without feeling attached to the outcome. Imagine not personalizing the outcome of your efforts and not having your identity and self-esteem riding on how things turn out. Imagine not needing things to go a certain way to feel good about who you are (or to avoid feeling bad about yourself). Imagine being neither overly attached to achieving success nor avoiding failure.

Imagine relaxing about the unknown and the uncertainty of how things will turn out, releasing any need to control how things go because of fear of the outcome. Imagine finding a healthy balance between putting forth your very best effort and then letting go of the outcome, reminding yourself of the saying: *Take care of the present moment and the future will take care of itself.* Imagine not taking everything quite so seriously. Imagine saying *So what?* to your fear that things may not turn out right.

Notice the different feelings that arise as you let go of your attachment to the outcomes and learn to surrender the need to control how things turn out. See if you can practice this approach to reducing the pressure and stress that you have been feeling around public speaking or performing, and possibly in some other areas of your life as well.

CHAPTER THIRTY-TWO

Cultivating Trust in Yourself and Others

WHEN WE ARE EXPERIENCING EXCESSIVE FEAR AND ANXIETY, we are having great difficulty trusting. We do not trust in ourselves, in others, or in the situation we are facing. We lack belief and faith that we can handle the challenge we face, that others will be supportive and helpful, and that the situation will turn out okay.

Instead, we experience doubt—we doubt our own ability to meet the challenge at hand, and we doubt others' willingness to be kind, accepting, and supportive. We doubt that things will turn out okay for us, and we may even wonder if we will survive the experience intact.

In fact, we may hold a belief that things will turn out far from okay—that we will have some awful experience and will suffer deep and lasting hurt, psychologically and socially. We do not have faith in our capacity to handle mishaps or to bounce back from difficult or unpleasant experiences. Our lack of faith in ourselves, in others, and in our situation deepens our worry and anxiety and often leaves us feeling lost and alone.

For many of us, when it comes to public speaking or performing, it has become easier to avoid moving outside of our comfort zone than take the risk that things may go badly. In fact, we may be highly risk-adverse when it comes to speaking or performing and we may find ourselves doing all we can to avoid situations where we will be asked to speak or perform publicly. Without a fundamental trust that we are safe and that things will turn out okay for us, it often feels way too risky to venture outside of our comfort zone.

Instead, we try to protect ourselves as much as possible from what may feel like "the enemy"—the thing that makes us feel so deeply frightened and vulnerable. Of course, it is natural to not trust an enemy and to not feel safe when we venture into enemy territory. Instead, it is adaptive to be on guard and stay vigilant whenever we have to confront the enemy, doing all we can to protect ourselves from potential danger. When we experience public speaking or performing as though it were our enemy, and as though we are facing potential danger each time we approach a speaking or performing event, our distrust of it deepens.

At an earlier time in our lives, some of us had more belief and faith in ourselves when it came to public speaking or performing, but we somehow lost it along the way. Others of us never felt safe and secure about speaking or performing, even from a very early age. Many of us have had one or more emotionally charged experiences with speaking or performing that took us off guard and frightened us terribly as we unexpectedly felt a deep sense of vulnerability and loss of control.

The memories of these experiences have been imprinted in our mind and nervous system, continuing to trigger a primal fear and an intense feeling of threat and danger each time we venture toward speaking or performing. Most of us never fully recovered from the trauma of those initial feelings of vulnerability and loss of control and have remained on guard ever since. We never want to be taken by surprise ever again by such an intensely frightening and overwhelming experience.

Our fear, anxiety, and worry seem to help us feel protected from the possibility of being caught off guard again. We are always prepared and ready for the worst, so we will never be surprised. While we want to trust, and to believe and have faith that we are safe, trusting also makes us feel uneasy, as we do not want any surprises. So, paradoxically, we feel safer holding on to our fear, anxiety, and worry and keeping our guard up—just in case.

Many of us had never encountered such deep feelings of fear and vulnerability, or felt so out of control, until we had one of these traumatic experiences. Prior to this we may have felt generally secure and confident in our ability to handle life's challenges. When we came upon a situation with speaking or performing that unexpectedly—and intensely—overwhelmed our capacity to cope, and also exposed our deeper vulnerability, we found ourselves losing trust in ourselves and our ability to handle this type of challenge. We lost the feeling of being able to count on ourselves and came to doubt that we would ever be able to handle situations of speaking or performing with confidence and ease. We have carried this self-doubt with us ever since.

Many of us have also lost our trust in others and in most, if not all, situations that require us to publicly speak or perform. Because we have felt so vulnerable around speaking or performing, we have projected much mistrust onto others and onto the speaking or performing situation itself. Our guard is up to protect ourselves from what we believe will be harsh judgment by others if they see our fear and vulnerability. We are afraid to relax and let our guard down. Instead, we maintain an invisible wall between ourselves and others, and brace ourselves for the worst that may come in the situation.

Trust is not easily regained once we have lost it. Believing in ourselves once again does not come easily after we have lost confidence in ourselves. Taking a leap of faith seems scary indeed when we have learned to keep ourselves safe by staying within our comfort zone as much as possible. Trusting in others and in the situation seems risky. We might get hurt if we relax and let our guard down—we might miss seeing something unexpected that could lead us to feel a loss of control.

While our fear, anxiety, and worry serve to protect us in facing the unknown, this self-protective stance also obstructs us from developing the deeper, more fundamental trust in ourselves, in others, and in the situation that is required to gain confidence as we face our public speaking or performing challenges.

In fact, in order to heal from this fear, relaxing and letting down our guard is the very thing we need to do. We need to let go of the fear-based memories and associations linked to past experiences with speaking or performing and become grounded in a fundamental feeling of safety and security. To heal deeply and fully requires that we cultivate trust and belief in ourselves and others. It requires that we let go of our self-protective stance and take a leap of faith as we approach the uncertain and unknown in the challenges we face.

It means developing trust in our capacity to handle whatever comes our way, especially now that we better understand this challenge and are developing skills to manage it more effectively. It means learning to have trust in the basic goodness of others and the inherent safety in the speaking or performing situation itself.

To let down our guard and let go of our fear, anxiety, and worry can feel risky, as we never want to be caught off guard again by such deep feelings of vulnerability and loss of control. But to keep our guard up and be braced for bad things to happen almost guarantees we will continue to be afraid and continue to suffer.

Letting go of fear and taking a leap of faith into the unknown often becomes easier when we have a belief in a power greater than ourselves, whether it be a belief in God or some other universal force. When we surrender to a power greater than ourselves, we feel an almost immediate sense of relief and support.

Rather than shouldering the burden of fear on our own, and trying to control what is beyond our control, we can reach to a higher power and ask for safety and assistance as we venture into the unknown. We can turn over our fear and uncertainty to this higher power and trust that we are being guided and supported. We can begin to trust that we are being given these challenges to help us grow and evolve to our highest potential.

This guidance and support is there for us at all times and, when we connect with this higher power, we become more able to relax, let go, and trust we will be given all that we need to meet our challenges. We are more easily able to develop trust in ourselves, in others, and in the challenges we face when we feel guided and supported by a power greater than ourselves.

Guiding Intention: I connect with a power greater than myself, and trust I am being guided and supported and will be given all that I need to meet life challenges.

Affirmative Thought: I am growing in my trust in myself, in others, and in my speaking (or performing) experiences.

Practice: Close your eyes and spend a few minutes relaxing as you breathe slowly and deeply. Reflect on the difficulty you may have experienced with feeling trust in yourself, in others, and in the speaking or performing situations you have faced.

Feel the sensation of being on guard and bracing yourself as you anticipate a negative experience. Observe how your fear, anxiety, and worry form a protective shield around you so you are prepared for the worst and won't be surprised by an unexpected feeling of loss of control. Notice how your feelings of fear and guardedness create a wall between you and others, keeping you separate and distant. Notice any discomfort or risk you may feel at the thought of letting down your guard and fully letting go of your fear, anxiety, and worry as you approach speaking or performing situations.

Now, shake off any uncomfortable feelings and take a few deep, relaxing breaths. Imagine very slowly and cautiously letting down your guard and releasing the fear, anxiety, and worry in small, incremental amounts. Imagine taking a leap of faith, and see yourself slowly and steadily developing trust and belief in yourself, in others, and in the situation, knowing you are truly safe and no harm will come to you.

Imagine calling upon a higher power for guidance and support and trusting that you will be given all the strength and wisdom you need to meet the challenge at hand. Imagine wiping the slate clean of earlier experiences that led to feelings of fear and mistrust and approaching any future speaking or performing situations with a relaxed, open, and trusting feeling. Consciously practice this new approach each time you face a speaking or performing challenge so your trust in yourself, in others, and in the situation will deepen and strengthen over time.

Real Life
Stories

I HAVE BEEN FORTUNATE TO WORK WITH MANY WONDERFUL PEOPLE over the last eleven years since I started offering workshops and coaching to people who suffer from the fear of public speaking and performing. I have been impressed by the high caliber of the people whom I have met who struggle with this fear. They are smart, capable, interesting, and talented in many ways. They are also very likeable and friendly people who are kind, sensitive, and caring. I have sometimes joked that if you had to belong to a club, this is a good one to belong to, as you are in the company of some amazing people who bring so much to the table.

Unfortunately, though, many of the people I have encountered have underestimated and second-guessed themselves and have not recognized just how much value they have to offer. They have often felt their confidence and belief in themselves adversely affected by their struggle with this fear. While most of us would do just about anything to not have this fear, it is important to fully appreciate your capability and value as the person you are, rather than judging yourself on your challenges with speaking or performing.

I have worked with many hundreds of clients that are just like you—people who have struggled for years with this fear and know well the feelings and experiences that go along with this challenge. They have worked steadily to gain knowledge and skills to move beyond this fear and have made much progress.

While they may still feel some anxiousness when asked to speak or per-form, they no longer feel panic, dread, or overwhelm. In fact, many clients report feeling more confident and empowered as they build upon their successes in managing this fear, and some even report feeling excited when asked to speak or perform because it is an opportunity to strengthen their new skills and build further on their successes.

Many clients also report applying the principles and skills they have learned in working on this fear to other areas of their lives, benefiting in ways beyond what they ever imagined. Many have also spoken of an unexpected and far-reaching gain as they created a more positive relationship with themselves and learned to not be so hard on themselves in many ways. By working on this challenge using a deeper and more holistic approach, they have gained greater self-awareness, self-acceptance, and self-appreciation and have learned to support themselves in ways that serve them in all areas of their lives.

I would now like to introduce you to a few of my workshop and coaching clients who have chosen to share their inspiring stories with you. I have also received many inspirational stories over the years from people who have benefited from reading my first book, *In The SpotLight*, and applying methods they learned from the book, and I will share one of those stories with you as well. While I have changed some identifying information to protect confidentiality, I share their stories as they have told them, in their own voices.

Harry O., age 55, professor of molecular botany

I HAVE BEEN A PROFESSOR AT AN IVY LEAGUE UNIVERSITY FOR many years, and no one knew I harbored a dark secret. By all external signs, most people would consider me successful in both teaching and research. However, students and colleagues weren't aware of my intense discomfort at speaking before an audience. I managed to keep my feelings hidden, thinking it was something I had to deal with; but, after more than twenty years, my affliction became worse and I found I was having difficulty hiding it anymore.

Even short introductions of guest speakers became a problem. Speaking in front of others caused me to lose sleep, to be anxious, and to waste time worrying. I turned away opportunities to speak, which was having a negative effect on my career.

I bottomed out when, after serving for several years as a Dean in the University, I was introduced by a colleague as a super-accomplished professor. With that introduction, I feared that my talk didn't match my accomplishments. During the talk, I experienced terrifying sensations—I was having trouble breathing, my voice became strained, I was sweating, and my knees felt weak. These feelings never happened to me before and they frightened me. I bolted to avoid humiliation—I actually left the room! Realizing what I had done, I came up with a plausible excuse as to why I had to leave and I promptly returned.

No one ever said anything and even now I don't know what people thought. However, I knew there was a serious problem and I began to think seriously about quitting a job I loved.

I struggled with this problem for a long time and I read several books, which were useless to me. Finally I came across Janet's book and I devoured it. Her book gave examples of other people with the same fear and the book really resonated with me. I found myself in its pages and it seemed that she knew how I felt because she'd been there. Reading the book made me feel that maybe there was hope and I didn't have to quit.

I attended a workshop with about a dozen people of all ages. I was embarrassed that I needed to be there and I considered not revealing who I really was. As people described themselves and the reasons why they were there, I learned that everyone was bright, every story was compelling, and they were all suffering like I was. Many were also highly accomplished and their fear of public speaking meant lost opportunities that limited their careers. I was humbled by their stories, and I no longer felt the need to hide my identity when it was my turn.

During the workshop the group members talked openly about the fear that was haunting them. We came together and tried to help one another. I was amazed at how much we accomplished in just two days! I learned how to stop judging myself so harshly and comparing myself to others. I learned to stop dwelling on parts of my talk that I wish I had done better. I came to realize that others cannot perceive our inner anxiety and discomfort in the way we are experiencing it and that we appear much calmer than we feel inside—this was an important revelation for me.

Rather than looking for a cure, I learned how to manage the anxiety so it wouldn't get out of hand. For example, I learned that when I felt a physical reaction coming on—to let it happen, observe it, and even regard it as a companion rather than an enemy. I learned to not feed my fertile imagination of what might occur. I learned that if I fixate on it and try to fight it, the reaction will get stronger and become a major focus of attention. By accepting my physical symptoms, I realized they can no longer surprise and terrorize me.

Another thing I learned to do was to focus on the message rather than myself. If we concentrate on getting the message across, we become less important and our attention shifts from ourselves to what we're trying to convey, which benefits our audience and lessens our anxiety.

I also took an advanced workshop and some refresher courses with Janet. Eventually, with more practice of the skills I was learning in a friendly and supportive environment, I felt the fear of public speaking abate naturally. I realized I no longer feared the fear. I also learned to lighten up and not take myself or this fear so seriously.

About three months after my first workshop with Janet, I was scheduled to give my first keynote talk at a conference in New Zealand. I was both eager and anxious to practice what I had been taught to do to manage my fear. I bought Janet's CD to relax and I also had a phone session to allow her to coach me one-on-one before the talk. To warm up, I practiced what I had learned in less threatening talks and tried to stay calm.

Interestingly, a Nobel Prize winner was the speaker who went before me when I did my keynote! What helped was that I considered that he might also be suffering from his own pressures. For example, he might have worried about whether his talk was appropriate for a Nobel Prize winner. However, I admit that his talk did cause me some consternation.

My talk was in the morning, and I walked the thirty minutes to the conference to relax. My host, who was gracious, inadvertently put me on edge just before my talk when he said to me that now we would see if I was worth all the money it took to get me there! Nevertheless, I felt really comfortable giving the talk, which was acknowledged by my host and others. One of the greatest compliments was a comment I heard from a student, who said she could follow my presentation and that she would like to talk with me because I seemed approachable. I knew then I had reached my audience. I also learned that I could allow myself to accept the praise.

It is no surprise that many of the lessons Janet has offered to help my public speaking are entirely appropriate for the other challenges in my life. Learning to not be so hard on myself and having patience with myself wherever I am at are pieces of the advice that has a new meaning for me now. I still apply the lessons I have learned from Janet to my life in general.

In one newsletter I recall Janet wrote a piece about how often we wish we were further along than we are. She advised that we take a slow, deep breath and say something to ourselves like: *I know I would prefer to be further up the river and closer to where those other boats are, but I also understand that my boat is here in this spot right now, and it better serves me to accept where my boat is at this moment rather than fight it. Then I can work on slowly making my way up the river so I can get closer to where I want to be.* I now understand more of what she meant.

Greg J., age 40, vice president, insurance industry

WHEN I FIRST ATTENDED JANET'S WEEKEND WORKSHOP MY ONLY goal was to eliminate, or at least significantly reduce, the anxiety and nervousness I felt when I spoke in public. For me, this was an odd struggle, considering I was often in a position of conducting meetings or giving presentations. Somehow, the frequency of speaking in a public setting didn't do much to mitigate the anxiety I felt before—and many times during—a meeting or presentation.

During the workshop I started to understand that anxiety around public speaking was not usually a stand-alone condition but often a symptom of underlying causes. This was an important discovery for me because tackling my uneasiness around public speaking has led me to multiple victories.

For example, I used to be fairly self-critical and judgmental about my presentations or how I conducted a meeting. Instead of looking at the presentation or meeting based on what others got out of it, I looked at it as a "performance." It was more about how I came across than about the content or the impact of the material. That, of course, is a no-win proposition. If you start with judgmental optics, you can always find something about yourself or your presentations to criticize.

What I came to realize, through the weekend workshop and subsequent coaching sessions with Janet, is that I was in a state of ongoing judgment of myself. Not just during or after a presentation, but in many areas of my life where I felt deficient in some way. When I started to replace self-judgment with self-support (positive self-talk, visualization, drawing on past successes), my anxiety before a meeting or presentation eased up and gave way to more confidence. I also began to see the same results in other areas of my life that have nothing to do with presentations or meetings. It's as if my brain needed some open space to house healthier and more productive emotions.

Another issue I've struggled with over the years is the need to control. I learned that if I apply a similar formula and replace control with acceptance, I can let go of my need to control and accept the flow of things with less stress and more grace. I never realized how much stress I inflicted on myself by trying to control my outer world. For me, accepting the reality of things going differently from what I had planned or expected—and trusting that things will ultimately turn out fine—was a major victory in my personal evolution toward being a more flexible and less stressed human being.

Prior to attending Janet's workshop and having coaching sessions with her, I had gone to a couple of workshops on how to give better presentations. I also attended a couple of Toastmasters meetings. All of these things were helpful to some extent, but, for me, none of them addressed the root cause of my presentation anxiety.

It has been very helpful to understand how interconnected my personal qualities are with my public speaking anxiety and to learn to embrace my unique combination of strengths. This has helped me to not only reduce my public speaking anxiety, but the benefits have also spilled over to my life as a parent, boss, husband, friend . . . you name it! I am amazed at how my frustration with public speaking has opened so many doors for personal growth.

Michelle S., age 43, development director

I HAVE HAD ANXIETY AROUND PUBLIC SPEAKING FOR QUITE A while. I became particularly challenged by it this past year after taking a new job that required me to present much more often than I had to in the past. When I first started to present at this new job, I was very anxious. I spent too much time ruminating about the presentations. But I was also determined not to let my fear interfere with my goals.

So I contacted Janet to learn some effective strategies to manage my fear. In addition to phone coaching sessions, I spent a lot of time reviewing Janet's first book and listening to her CD. I created and frequently reviewed a list of self-affirmations and coping statements. I tried different relaxation techniques, including yoga. For many nights before a presentation, I visualized myself talking confidently in front of my audience. It was a lot of work but was well worth it as I began to notice my anticipatory anxiety lessen and my confidence grow.

Over the last year, I've successfully completed a bunch of presentations in front of various audiences. While I still have some anxiety before certain presentations, it's much more manageable now. And I can finally put my presentations in perspective; I no longer view them as momentous events. In looking back over the last year, the most important lessons I've learned include the following:

- Don't fight the symptoms. Just acknowledge your body's reaction and let it be okay.
- Remember that presenting doesn't pose any danger; your fear won't hurt you.
- Don't judge yourself. Be gentle with yourself.
- Be as prepared as you can before you present but also learn to go with the flow. You cannot control everything.
- Take the focus off of yourself. Instead, focus on what you can give to your audience. The audience isn't thinking about you nearly as much as you think they are.
- Don't take yourself too seriously. Remember to smile. Put your presentation in perspective.
- You're going to be okay, no matter what.

Adam B., age 39, marketing executive

ALONG WITH MOST PEOPLE, I HAD A HEALTHY FEAR OF PUBLIC speaking for as long as I can remember. I remember even in high school feeling very nervous about a certain class speech or about a part in a show. However, I was able to do those things and just accept my nervousness.

It was when I started to work that I became more concerned with how I appeared when I spoke. It was a gradual process, but I began to develop a fear of appearing nervous. When my voice shook, I thought people saw me as weak or unprofessional and that it would hamper my ability to rise in the organization. And the further I rose, the more I became afraid of how I would look and sound as I nervously delivered presentations.

It was in one meeting, as I delivered a presentation to a small group, that I experienced something totally new. My heart raced so quickly that I felt truly panicked. I could not even get a sentence out. Were it not for my manager seeing that I needed some help and saying a few words while I collected myself, I'm not sure what I would have done.

From that day on, I experienced that panic in many different situations. And I began to fear that panic, to the point where for months before the presentation I would feel only dread. I would rehearse my presentations literally dozens of times to make myself feel better.

The panic did not always happen when I presented, but the fear of it was always with me. It got so bad that even participating in meetings (even on the phone!) became a challenge. I don't know if it held me back in terms of my career, but it certainly was making work a very unpleasant experience for me. And the higher I rose, the more presentations I had to do, and the worse it got.

As soon as I found out I had to give a presentation it would feel like a heavy weight was sitting on my chest. I felt scared, but it came out as anger that I had to give the presentation, and often that anger would find its way into my interactions with my family and friends.

During the presentation, my heart raced and my breath grew very short. It felt almost impossible to concentrate on what I had to say, and it felt as though I was retreating within myself. To say I was "paralyzed by fear" might be too strong, but my ability to function appropriately for the given situation was very much diminished. I felt like I had lost control over my own body. And because my fear stemmed from appearing nervous to others, and what they might think of me, the cycle kept feeding itself.

While I would have liked to avoid public speaking situations, I was afraid that the avoidance itself would show how nervous I was, so I didn't end up avoiding many of these situations. My main way of dealing with my fear was over-rehearsing. I spent countless hours rehearsing. It gave me a short-term lift and made me believe that everything was going to be okay, but that feeling didn't last long. As the day of the presentation grew closer, I sometimes rehearsed my talk five times a day for a full week.

A combination of things that I learned from Janet has helped me. I have used her CD to practice relaxation and deep breathing. This has been a big help before a presentation and has allowed me to feel in control of my own body. From her book and personal coaching, I understand now that my primary focus needs to be on my audience and what they get out of my presentation. Learning to take the focus off myself has been very helpful. I remind myself that almost everybody gets nervous. I remember examples of seeing other people get nervous and realize that my feelings about them or their presentation were not diminished by their nervousness. This helps me challenge the idea that showing nervousness will be perceived as a weakness. I have also learned to remind myself of my successes and forgive myself for my mistakes and imperfections.

I was asked to emcee a three-day forum run by my CEO. This meant that much of what I did on stage could not be rehearsed and had to be an impromptu reaction to what was going on during the forum at that given time. In addition, I had to deliver a prepared presentation and had to host an awards dinner. I was basically on stage constantly for three days.

In our coaching, the first thing Janet reminded me of was to focus on my purpose. As the emcee, my purpose was to help the audience navigate the conference and also feel comfortable in a room full of other executives. That really helped me switch my focus away from myself. We also discussed a shift in my attitude, and I pushed myself to have a good attitude about the event and see it as an opportunity (which it really was) to get my name and face out in front of an important crowd. This also helped me to stay in good spirits before the event. During the event, I used the breathing exercises I had learned to keep myself calm and really focused on the agenda and the audience. For the most part, it went very well. I felt very relaxed at the podium and really enjoyed it. I was even funny, which I was not expecting!

Ironically, the one part that I tripped up on in terms of presentation was delivering a speech during the awards dinner with the use of teleprompters. I found it hard to read and sound natural, so it made me very self-conscious and I tripped over some words. However, I forgave myself, moved on, and did not dwell on this. All in all it was a great experience. I also did it again a year later and had another good experience.

I have gained a great deal of benefit from my work with Janet. I think it has opened my eyes to broader issues that I have with control and the need to let go of trying to control every situation. I have learned that I cannot control everything in life. I cannot control the reactions of people in my audience, and trying to control this makes me even more nervous.

I have worked hard (and Janet reminds me) to just let it go and trust things will be okay. When things don't go as I had planned, I try to see my reaction to it as a learning opportunity and challenge. This is something I am still working on (and may be for a very long time), but it is so helpful and has really opened my eyes to how sometimes I avoid stepping out of my comfort zone and adhere to rigid routines because I am afraid of losing that control.

I am now for the first time realizing that there is a lot of excitement and happiness that is possible for me as I learn to let go of control. It gives me a lot of incentive to press on with this even though at times it can feel like a tough challenge.

Sheila V., age 52, singer and office manager for family-owned businesses

I HAVE ALWAYS BEEN CLASSIFIED AS SHY, A LABEL THAT I WISH hadn't been given to me at a very young age. It took years for me to overcome this debilitating condition that I felt was actually a handicap. I went through all my school years feeling less than adequate and definitely not strong and courageous.

I had my first experience with panic attacks in tenth grade, which was a traumatic year for me related to some very upsetting social situations and left me in a pile of rubble, emotionally speaking. After this occurrence I started to notice that I was having trouble in many aspects of the social scene.

My father was our band director and I found myself having panic attacks as I tried to continue performing in the band. This caused me much grief and I felt that something was mentally wrong with me at many points. As the years progressed I became stronger, especially spiritually, as I continued to work through shyness issues. I felt I had overcome the condition for the most part.

Currently, I have been experiencing change-of-life. Through some researching, I have come to learn that many women who don't resolve specific emotional issues earlier on will find themselves knee deep in them again at this time. The anxiety came back and was so highly charged I had to stop singing for a while with our Praise Band at church and also bowed out of many social and family functions. On a scale of one to ten, the anxiety I experienced was off the charts. I recall fleeing many times from specific events and declining to sing a special at church, it was that intense. Oftentimes I'd go ahead and sing, only to end up out in the lobby trying to calm my body symptoms down.

I don't feel I coped well with this challenge. I just toughed my way through it, suffering the entire time and trying to hide it. For quite some time the fight or flight response always led to my fleeing. Rarely did I choose to fight this intense negative energy inside me. When I'd get home, to a safe place, the feeling would leave, but it took getting home and away from the threatening situation for me to feel any sense of peace.

The symptoms I would experience included: pounding heart, breathlessness, extreme cotton mouth, sweaty palms and feet, pains in various parts of my body, and skin flushing on my chest and neck. I would even have twitching muscles during extreme times of panic. Sometimes my chest would hurt and I would have a pain in my shoulder blade area and it would feel like I was having a heart attack. It was very frightening when this would happen, as this can be a symptom of a heart attack. The most severe symptoms I experienced involved feeling detached, dizzy and disoriented. The best way I can describe it is a feeling of not even being in your body—like you've left.

Janet's book was a godsend for me, which led me to sign up for her No More Stage Fright workshop. In suffering from this fear, it's easy to go through all of this silently, with no hope in sight. Attending Janet's workshop, I learned that I'm not alone. Being in a room full of people who have also experienced this fear is so freeing.

I continue to read through her book when I need to regroup and also use her CD regularly, especially the relaxation tracks. My body is learning what it feels like to be relaxed and it's a process that has to be repeated over and over. I listen to the positive affirmations on my way to church, being this is an area where I have had the most trouble as I attempted to minister through music. I also frequently read through specific areas of my workbook from the workshop training. I also had a coaching session with Janet over the phone and it was very helpful.

Although I am not totally free from this condition, I have noticed major improvement. "Feel the fear but do it anyway" has been a message of great value to me. It's amazing that people never know I'm nervous when I'm singing or playing an instrument. I get out my video tape periodically from the workshop and honestly cannot tell I'm nervous. And during those workshop exercises that were videotaped, I was extremely nervous with all of the above symptoms present.

I'm learning to not be afraid of the symptoms and to realize when I move into a second fear—meaning I start to fear the fear. I have learned that when my mind starts to focus on the symptoms, it creates more fear. I often ask myself a powerful question that Janet posed to the group during the workshop: "What would it feel like to let go of this feeling?" I get an immediate sense of relaxation when I let go and quit fighting it.

I have also changed my diet for the better and have gotten back to regular exercise. I noticed that eliminating caffeine made a big difference in reducing my anxiety.

Thankfully, I have had many victories. When these occur I'm literally in my car driving home from church praising God for the freedom I experienced. Victory is on the horizon for me, and it's taken many steps to achieve it. Purchasing Janet's book and attending her workshop have been two powerful steps on my path toward freedom.

Learning ways to overcome performance anxiety have also helped me incredibly in other areas of my life. I came to realize that life is not all about me and that people are not focusing on me, nor are they oftentimes even aware that I have entered a room. Prior to this I sometimes felt like I was always on stage—the stage of life—and it was frightening.

The tools I learned through Janet have assisted me in many areas of life as I move through specific social settings that formerly made me very uncomfortable. My personal gifts are to be shared, and to be selfishly withdrawing and not sharing what I have to offer does not benefit anyone. This fact even applies to life in general. When we withdraw from speaking or socializing, we aren't letting our light shine and we ultimately allow our light to be snuffed out.

Figuratively speaking, Janet had the ability to light my candle again. It's up to me how much that light grows, but through her compassion to help others I know my light is going to be growing more and more as I continue to apply the principles of overcoming this seemingly debilitating condition. I've often stated this fact as I've progressed through the valley of fear—*If Sheila can overcome fear, anyone can!!!*

Luke P., age 44, managing partner, financial services

MY FEAR OF PUBLIC SPEAKING EVOLVED OVER THE YEARS STARTING when I was a little kid and had to give an oral report. I specifically remember as a ten-year-old losing my place on an oral report and basically crumbling. That started the cycle where I would avoid these types of presentations, and all types of performances in front of people in general.

Over the last ten years, I have been called upon to give presentations at work and they were always a struggle before attending Janet's workshops and engaging her in one-on-one coaching. I remember one presentation in particular where it was apparent that I was nervous and this realization only made me even more nervous. Although I have achieved good success academically and professionally—receiving my undergraduate and masters degrees from a top-ten school and then going on to run a global financial business and now my own firm—I believe this fear has hindered me and led to missed opportunities.

In the past, I had done my best to avoid any and all situations of public speaking and had others do the talking for me when possible. It was very frustrating to have my message delivered by someone else, as I know I could have done it better. I have missed meetings, put them off, or changed the formats—all to avoid speaking.

I read Janet's book, had one-on-one coaching, and attended two of her workshops. One of the most helpful things I learned to do is to stay in the moment and acknowledge my fear. I don't believe my fear is ever going to go away fully, but I know that if I can recognize it and understand it, then I can control it better.

I came to understand that many successful people suffer from this fear and only a blessed few actually enjoy public speaking or are naturally good at it. I also learned to not take myself so seriously. I'm not going to die from this and the world isn't going to come to an end. This has been important to remember, as this fear can make us lose perspective.

The best example of applying what I had learned after working with Janet is a presentation I made to about 150 people about 9/11. I stayed in the moment, was extremely well-prepared, and practiced relaxed breathing. I was pleased with how well I did with this challenge and I received positive feedback afterwards.

Since then, my presentations have gotten better and better, and I have even gotten to the point where I have conducted finance seminars for some of the top firms in the world. I have my own conversational style and have employed this as a way to communicate better and to stay on familiar ground. I may never be great at public speaking, but I am going to be the best that I can be, and that's all right.

The progress I have made with public speaking has benefited other areas of my life as well. It has allowed me to speak up when I have something to say (sometimes I don't even want to stop talking now) and has allowed me to become a better communicator across the board. I stick to the matter at hand when speaking with people on all levels and stay in the moment.

It has been said that most people would rather be lying in the casket than giving the eulogy but I see things very differently now. I believe one of the most important things in life is communication and all of my efforts have allowed me to communicate much, much better.

Claire B., age 36, marketing executive

MY PUBLIC SPEAKING JOURNEY STARTED IN GRADE SCHOOL. I was afraid to speak up in class. When teachers posed questions and asked for volunteers, I knew the answers but was always too shy to raise my hand. I did okay in college with public speaking but again never spoke up voluntarily. I would scan every syllabus for classes to make sure there were none or few public speaking requirements.

It was in graduate school when I knew I needed help. During a group presentation that I was very well prepared for, I had a full blown panic attack. It was so bad that I walked out of the room. There was nothing extraordinary about the speech. It was a combination of my fear and other stresses that were occurring in my life at that time. It was one of the most shameful experiences in my life.

After college my career choice, marketing, was one where I needed to give many presentations. I was always so happy when they were over with but knew there was always another one around the corner. Before one important speech, I ended up asking my boss to give it because I was just too nervous, and then I knew it was time to get some help. I searched online and found Janet Esposito. Quite simply, she helped me change my life. I found her book, workshops, and phone coaching invaluable.

After reading her book, I couldn't wait to go to Janet's workshop. I remember walking into her workshop and feeling like I had known her for years. The weekend was a perfect blend of discussing the fear, hands-on exercises, and helpful techniques. I went to all of the workshops that she hosted on the West Coast. It was wonderful working with people in the workshops who shared the same fear, and it was nice to see I was not alone.

I have also found Janet's phone coaching very helpful. She has an amazing way of understanding what you need to get out of the sessions over the phone. The phone coaching was so valuable that I set calls up every month. I found myself getting help with not only public speaking but other areas in my life as well.

After years of working with Janet, I have given many speeches without the terror that I had before. However, I always need to practice deep relaxation techniques before every speech, such as meditation, yoga, massages, and hot baths. The fear never goes away, but I am able to manage it better.

Mark P., age 49, ad executive

THERE WAS A TIME IN MY LIFE WHEN I THOUGHT I WOULD have to change careers even after investing years and years to build what was rapidly becoming a successful advertising agency with my two partners. The truth is, I was terrified of speaking in public—to the extent that even presenting a campaign or pitching new business to a group would throw me into the deep end of the anxiety pool.

The night before these presentations, I would lie in bed as raw, ice-cold fear would shoot through my body. I would play the whole scene out in my head, over and over and over, and the more it played out in my head, the worse it got. This constant fear was sucking the life out of me.

And then I met Janet—first by reading a story about her and her company in an in-flight magazine, and then by calling her the next day and working closely with her through phone coaching sessions. I applied all of the tools she outlined in her book and checked in with her before major presentations. Without question, this experience has transformed me. I can now make a presentation or pitch new business with total confidence—completely in control of my emotions.

I have progressed even to the point that the fear has become such a nonissue that I began to work with Janet on improving other areas of my life, using similar techniques and approaches.

I can't express enough thanks and appreciation for what I have learned from Janet—her approach is highly personal, caring, and authentic, and I never would have made it out of some of those deep, dark holes without her.

Elizabeth B., age 30, administrative professional, Government of Canada

THOUGH I FELT THE PRESSURE WHEN I ATTENDED PUBLIC speaking competitions at school in my youth, I nonetheless excelled at doing this. However, in college, my public speaking anxiety increased, as I was no longer in the safe and familiar small town school environment. This culminated in what I call the "frog voice" incident.

I had a part-time job as a waitress while I was in college. I provided great customer service and frequently received positive comment cards from customers. Accordingly, I had developed a reputation of being a star employee with management.

One day, the management team had dinner in my serving section. I was intimidated since I felt I had to meet their expectations and deliver (though I already had!). For some reason, my confidence spiraled and the words coming out of my mouth were choked and garbled. I felt dizzy and flushed. Their inquisitive looks mortified me as I muttered something about having a sore throat. I just couldn't get my bearings back.

This incident affected me profoundly. I felt that I couldn't trust myself any more in public speaking events since "frog voice" might come out of nowhere and humiliate me. I started choosing courses in college that didn't require oral presentations and eventually gravitated toward distance education where the risk of oral presentations was nil. Then, as I embarked on my career as an administrative professional, I felt secure in the knowledge that oral presentations were not a part of my mandate.

Yet there soon came a time when I couldn't get out of a public speaking engagement at work. Though I made a few weak attempts to get out of it, I wanted to keep my fear of public speaking a secret, as I felt this was an embarrassing character flaw of mine. I had three months to "get my groove back" before the big day—that's where Janet's book came in. I related to it immediately. I knew how to be a good public speaker. I had just become so fearful of doing it!

I read Janet's book and took notes faithfully. What impacted me the most was reading that it really wasn't "all about me." My audience is not there to judge me. They are there to hear what I have to say, not how I say it. They are not expecting me to fail, nor to knock their socks off. This is not a competition. My audience is just like me—they have a life, and my presentation will not be the end all and be all.

On the morning of my big presentation, I got up four hours early to mentally prepare (a little excessive but that's what I needed to do!). I had laid out an action plan as per Janet's book. I had a good night's sleep (and did not stay up late worrying about my presentation), had a hearty breakfast, reread all my notes, did a lot positive self-talk and visualizations, rehearsed a few times (but not memorized!), meditated, and then walked out the door feeling somewhat good about myself.

And you know what, it worked! I got my groove back! My presentation was great—I was even relaxed enough to crack a few jokes and build a rapport with my audience. I was thrilled! And as per Janet's book, I forced myself to accept public speaking engagements as they arose, even though my instinct was to want to get out of them.

You can't imagine how pleased I was when I was able to stand in front of 200+ people to do a reading at my grandpa's funeral—something I would not have been able to do before reading Janet's book, which would have broken my heart!

Though I still feel like I want to shy away from speaking engagements, I know I can do it and I don't feel trapped by my fear anymore. This has been extremely liberating. I can't thank Janet enough. I highly recommend her book to anyone who has a fear of public speaking—it will change your life.

The Question of a "Quick Fix"

MANY OF US FIND OURSELVES LOOKING FOR A "QUICK FIX" to alleviate our suffering from the fear of public speaking or performing as quickly as possible and reduce the frustration and impatience we often feel while working on this challenge over time. I am not a big believer in "quick fixes." Having said that, I would like to make you aware of some methods offering the possibility for fast relief from fears and phobias, as well as other problems and challenges, which have gained respect.

While I have tried these methods a number of times myself, and have not personally experienced the quick and complete success that many claim is possible, I do think these methods have merit and are worth a try. For some people, these methods may provide a "quick fix" and transform their fear in a dramatic way; for others, these methods may have more subtle effects (as they did for me) or possibly no noticeable effects at all. You may want to investigate the following:

- Emotional Freedom Technique (EFT)—based on correcting subtle energy imbalances in our system that relate to negative emotions— visit **www.emofree.com**
- Eye Movement Desensitization and Reprocessing (EMDR)—based on a method of psychotherapy that has proved effective for the treatment of trauma—visit **www.emdria.org**
- Neurolinguistic Programming (NLP)—based on using the language

of the mind to consistently achieve specific and desired outcomes—
visit **www.nlp.com.**

While we may have much in common in our experiences with speaking or
performing anxiety, each of us is unique when it comes to the complex inter-
play between our physiological, emotional, mental, and spiritual makeup, as
well as all the influences that have shaped us over the years. What works for
some of us will not always work for all of us, which is why I like to offer a wide
range of principles and practices to choose from, where you are free to use
what works best for you and leave the rest (or possibly try something again at
a later time, as timing sometimes has a lot to do with what works well for us).

One of the things that I have used that some may consider a "quick fix"
has been the use of a beta blocker on an as-needed basis (e.g., Inderal, or Pro-
pranolol, which is commonly prescribed for performance anxiety). At other
times I have used natural remedies to help calm and support my body instead
of medication, depending upon my state of mind and body at the time and
the level of challenge I was facing.

While I am not a big proponent of using medication in general, I have
found that a beta blocker has been very helpful for me, and many others who
suffer from this fear, in providing additional support to ease the fight or flight
response that has been conditioned in the nervous system. It helps to calm and
desensitize the nervous system from being in an alarmed, agitated state when
speaking or performing. It can also help to recondition the fear response in
your nervous system over time so you feel less threatened and reactive when
speaking or performing.

Some people have not found beta blockers as helpful and have used an
anti-anxiety medication instead, or possibly a combination of both. If you
want to consider using medication, discuss the idea with your physician. It
is best to try it prior to a speaking or performing event so you can see how it
works with your body chemistry.

Some people may prefer not to use any medication at all, or they may
want to consider using a natural product to support their biochemistry, such
as an herbal remedy, an amino acid, homeopathy, or a Bach flower remedy. I

have tried a number of natural products that have worked well in my system and have taken the edge off of the feelings of anxiety and tension in both body and mind.

You can do some research on the natural products that may be helpful, though you should always check with a qualified and knowledgeable health practitioner to be sure whatever you want to try is a good choice for you, especially given the potential for interactions with other things you may be taking. Any medication or natural remedy is best used in conjunction with the other methods you have learned from this book, as part of a holistic body, mind, spirit approach.

CLOSING

Having this fear has not been easy for me, just as I know it has not been easy for you. Yet being able to share what I have learned along the way for the purpose of helping you, and the many others who share this fear, has given this challenge a deeper meaning in my life. I believe we can go beyond just surviving with this fear and truly learn to thrive. We can use this fear as an impetus for positive change and grow in ways that we may have never imagined.

There are so many lessons that can be learned on this journey. We can deepen our self-awareness and self-acceptance. We can learn to support and affirm ourselves and be gentler, kinder, and more patient with ourselves when we are struggling. We can accept our human vulnerabilities and let go of striving for perfection. We can let go of the feeling that we need to prove ourselves and learn to feel more comfortable in our own skin. We can learn to trust and believe in ourselves.

We can also learn to trust others more and feel safe being who we are when we are in the public eye. We can learn to connect more deeply with others and see people for who they really are rather than viewing them as our judges or critics. We can learn to be more other-focused instead of self-focused and to care more about contributing to others rather than trying to protect our own image or reputation. We can learn to tone down our ego concerns and not allow our self-esteem and self-worth to be so dependent upon our achievements and success or the acceptance and approval of others.

We can learn to let go of our strong need to be in control of ourselves and our circumstances. We can learn to relax and go with the flow. We can learn to trust things will turn out okay and learn helpful lessons from anything that does not go as we would like.

We can learn to be more attuned to our body and discover ways to ground and center ourselves when we feel agitated and off balance. We can learn to cultivate more consciousness in our mind and become less reactive and more adaptive in how we respond to our challenges. We can learn to maintain a positive focus and train our mind to be our ally. We can mature in many ways in response to this challenge—mentally, emotionally, and spiritually—and we can use this fear as a catalyst to grow and evolve as a person.

These are just some of the lessons to be learned in the process of stepping up to meet this challenge with a positive view and a determination to thrive rather than just survive. I hope you will use this book as your guide on this journey and refer to it often as you mine this challenge for the many valuable lessons it has to teach.

I thank you for your interest in reading this book, and I do hope you will apply many of the practices to make your journey easier and your experiences more positive and empowering. I would love to hear from you at any point to share your feedback, and your successes and challenges along the way. Please be sure to visit my web site at **www.performanceanxiety.com** to receive a checklist of valuable tips to help you create more calm and confidence before, during, and after your speaking or performing challenges.

I wish you ever-increasing personal growth and discovery as you share this amazing journey with me and many other kindred souls!

Warmest wishes,
Janet

Janet Esposito, MSW
P.O. Box 494
Bridgewater, CT 06752
860–210–1499
jesposito@performanceanxiety.com
www.performanceanxiety.com